D0106030

PENGUIN BOO

PURPLE COW

Seth Godin is the worldwide bestselling author of *Permission Marketing*, *Unleashing the Ideavirus* and *Survival Is Not Enough*. He is a renowned public speaker, has started several successful companies and is a contributing editor at *Fast Company* magazine. You can find him at www.sethgodin.com.

Purple Cow

Transform Your Business by Being Remarkable

Seth Godin

PENGUIN BOOKS

PENGUIN BOOKS

Published by the Penguin Group
Penguin Books Ltd, 80 Strand, London WC2R ORL, England
Penguin Group (USA) Inc., 375 Hudson Street, New York, New York 10014, USA
Penguin Group (Canada), 10 Alcorn Avenue, Toronto, Ontario, Canada M4V 3B2
(a division of Pearson Penguin Canada Inc.)
Penguin Ireland, 25 St Stephen's Green, Dublin 2, Ireland
(a division of Penguin Books Ltd)
Penguin Group (Australia), 250 Camberwell Road,
Camberwell, Victoria 3124, Australia (a division of Pearson Australia Group Pty Ltd)
Penguin Books India Pvt Ltd, 11 Community Centre
Panchsheel Park, New Delhi – 110 017, India
Penguin Group (NZ), cnr Airborne and Rosedale Roads, Albany,
Auckland 1310, New Zealand (a division of Pearson New Zealand Ltd)
Penguin Books (South Africa) (Pty) Ltd, 24 Sturdee Avenue,
Rosebank 2196, South Africa

Penguin Books Ltd, Registered Offices: 80 Strand, London WC2R ORL, England

www.penguin.com

First published in the United States of America by Portfolio 2003
First published in Great Britain by Michael Joseph 2004
Published in Penguin Books 2005

026

ISBN-13: 978–0–141–01640–5

www.greenpenguin.co.uk

IN MEMORY OF LIONEL POILANE,
Remarkable in Every Way.

Contents

Contents

CONTENTS

Contents

"Tastes like chicken"
isn't a compliment.

———

"Nobody laughs at
old jokes any more."

Max Godin

———

You are a post-consumption consumer.
You have everything you need,
and most everything you want.
Except time.

———

"Marketing is too important to be left to the
marketing department."

David Packard

———

"Everything that can be invented has been invented."

Charles H. Duell, 1899,
U.S. Commissioner of Patents

PURPLE
COW

NOT ENOUGH Ps

Marketers for years have talked about the five Ps of marketing. (There are more than five of them, but everyone has their favorite five.) Some of them include:

- Product
- Pricing
- Promotion
- Positioning
- Publicity
- Packaging
- Pass-along
- Permission

This is the marketing checklist: a quick way to make sure you've done your job, a way to describe how you're going to go about getting people to buy what the factory just made. If the elements are out of whack with each other (for example, puréed meals that you market to senior citizens but taste like baby food), then the marketing message is blurred and ultimately ineffective.

Marketing isn't guaranteed to work, but the way things used to be, if you got all your Ps right, you were more likely than not to succeed.

Something disturbing has happened, though. The Ps just aren't enough. This is a book about a new P, a P that is suddenly exceptionally important.

THE NEW P

The new P is "Purple Cow."

When my family and I were driving through France a few years ago, we were enchanted by the hundreds of storybook cows grazing on picturesque pastures right next to the highway. For dozens of kilometers, we all gazed out the window, marveling about how beautiful everything was.

Then, within twenty minutes, we started ignoring the cows. The new cows were just like the old cows, and what once was amazing was now common. Worse than common. It was boring.

Cows, after you've seen them for a while, are boring. They may be perfect cows, attractive cows, cows with great personalities, cows lit by beautiful light, but they're still boring.

A Purple Cow, though. Now *that* would be interesting. (For a while.)

The essence of the Purple Cow is that it must be remarkable. In fact, if "remarkable" started with a P, I could probably dispense with the cow subterfuge, but what can you do?

This book is about the why, the what, and the how of *remarkable*.

BOLDFACED WORDS AND GUTSY ASSERTIONS

Something **remarkable** is worth talking about. Worth noticing. Exceptional. New. Interesting. It's a Purple Cow. Boring stuff is invisible. It's a brown cow.

Remarkable marketing is the art of building things worth noticing right into your product or service. Not slapping on marketing as a last-minute add-on, but understanding that if your offering itself isn't remarkable, it's invisible.

The **TV-industrial complex** was the symbiotic relationship between consumer demand, TV advertising, and ever-growing companies that were built around investments in ever-increasing marketing expenditures.

The **post-consumption consumer** is out of things to buy. We have what we need, we want very little, and we're too busy to spend a lot of time researching something you've worked hard to create for us.

The **marketing department** takes a nearly finished product or service and spends money to communicate its special benefits to a target audience. This approach no longer works.

I believe we've now reached the point where we can no longer market directly to the masses. We've created a world where most products are invisible. Over the past two decades, smart business writers have pointed out that the dynamic of marketing is changing. Marketers have read and talked about those ideas, and even used some of them, but have maintained the essence of their old marketing strategies. The traditional approaches are now obsolete, though. One hundred years of marketing thought are gone. Alternative approaches aren't a novelty—they are all we've got left.

This is a book about why you need to put a Purple Cow into everything you build, why TV and mass media are no longer your secret weapons, and why the profession of marketing has been changed forever.

Stop advertising and start innovating.

Before, During, and After

Before Advertising, there was word of mouth. Products and services that could solve a problem got talked about and eventually got purchased.

The best vegetable seller at the market had a reputation, and her booth was always crowded.

During Advertising, the combination of increasing prosperity, seemingly endless consumer desire, and the power of television and mass media led to a magic formula: If you advertised directly to the consumer (every consumer), sales would go up.

A partnership with the right ad agency and the right banker meant you could drive a company to be almost as big as you could imagine.

After Advertising, we're almost back where we started. But instead of products succeeding by slow and awkward word of mouth, the power of our new networks allows remarkable ideas to diffuse through segments of the population at rocket speed.

As marketers, we know the old stuff isn't working. And we know why: because as consumers, we're too busy to pay attention to advertising, but we're desperate to find good stuff that solves our problems.

THE GREATEST THING SINCE SLICED BREAD

In 1912, Otto Frederick Rohwedder invented sliced bread. What a great idea: a simple machine that could take a loaf of bread and...slice it. The machine was a complete failure. This was the beginning of the advertising age, and that meant that a good product with lousy marketing had very little chance of success.

It wasn't until about twenty years later — when a new brand called Wonder started marketing sliced bread — that the invention caught on. It was the packaging and the advertising ("builds strong bodies twelve ways") that worked, not the sheer convenience and innovation of pre-slicing bread.

DID YOU NOTICE THE REVOLUTION?

Over the past twenty years, a quiet revolution has changed the way some people think about marketing.

Tom Peters took the first whack with *The Pursuit of Wow*, a visionary book that described why the only products with a future were those created by passionate people. Too often, big companies are scared companies, and they work to minimize any variation—including the good stuff that happens when people who care create something special.

Peppers and Rogers, in *The One to One Future*, took a simple truth—that it's cheaper to keep an old customer than it is to get a new one—and articulated the entire field of customer relationship management. They showed that there are only four kinds of people (prospects, customers, loyal customers, and former customers) and that loyal customers are often happy to spend more money with y

In *Crossing the Chasm*, Geoff Moore outlined how new products and new ideas move through a population. They follow a curve, beginning with innovators and early adopters, growing into the majority, and eventually reaching the laggards. While Moore focused on technology products, his insights about the curve apply to just about every product or service offered to any audience.

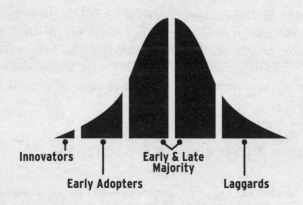

Innovators

Early Adopters

Early & Late Majority

Laggards

Moore's **idea diffusion curve** *shows how a successful business innovation moves — from left to right — and affects ever more consumers until it finally reaches everyone. The x-axis, along the bottom, shows the different groups an idea encounters over time, while the y-axis shows how many people are in each group.*

In *The Tipping Point*, Malcolm Gladwell clearly articulated how ideas spread through populations, from one person to another. In *Unleashing the Ideavirus*, I pushed this idea even further, describing how the most effective business ideas are the ones that spread.

And finally, in *Permission Marketing*, I outlined the ever-growing attention deficit that marketers face. I also discussed how companies win when they treat the attention of their prospects as an asset, not as a resource to be strip-mined and then abandoned.

At many companies, most of these proven ideas have been treated as novelties. My friend Nancy is the head of "new media" at one of the largest packaged-goods companies in the world. Guess what? She's in charge (she's a department of one) of all of these new ideas. "New media" has become a synonym for "no budget."

Instead of accepting that the old ways are fading away (fast), most companies with a product to market are treating these proven new techniques as interesting fads — worth another look but not worth using as the center of their strategy.

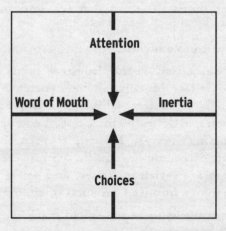

The squeeze play. Marketers can't get the word out because jaded consumers refuse to share their attention. Customers rely on their tried-and-true suppliers or on their network of smart friends instead of studying the ads on TV.

WHY YOU NEED THE PURPLE COW

Forty years ago, Ron Simek, owner of the Tombstone Tap (a bar named for the cemetery next door), decided to offer a frozen version of his pizza to his customers. It caught on, and before long, Tombstone Pizza was dominating your grocer's freezer. Kraft Foods bought the brand in 1986, advertised it like crazy, and made billions. This was a great American success story — invent a product everyone wants, advertise it to the masses, and make a lot of money.

This strategy didn't just work for pizza. It worked for almost everything in your house, including aspirin.

Imagine how much fun it must have been to be the first person to market aspirin. Here was a product that just about every person on earth needed and wanted. A product that was inexpensive, easy to try, and immediately beneficial.

Obviously, it was a big hit.

Today, a quick visit to the drugstore turns up: Advil, Aleve, Alka-Seltzer Morning Relief, Anacin, Ascriptin, Aspergum, Bayer, Bayer Children's, Bayer Regimen, Bayer Women's, BC, Bufferin, Cope, Ecotrin, Excedrin Extra Strength, Goody's, Motrin, Nuprin, St. Joseph, Tylenol, and of course, Vanquish. Within each of these brands, there are variations, sizes, and generics, adding up to more than a hundred products to choose from.

Think it's still easy to be an aspirin marketer?

If you developed a new kind of pain reliever, even one that was a bit better than all of those I just listed, what would you do?

The obvious answer, if you've got money and you believe in your product, is to spend all you've got to buy tons of national TV and print advertising.

You'll face a few problems, though. First you need people who want to buy a pain reliever. While it's a huge market, it's not everyone.

Once you find people who buy pain relievers, then you need people who want to buy a new kind. After all, plenty of people want the "original" kind, the kind they grew up with. If someone has found a convenient, trusted, effective pain reliever, he's probably not out there wasting time looking for a replacement.

Finally, you need to find the people willing to listen to you talk about your new pain reliever. The vast majority of folks are just too busy and will ignore you, regardless of how many ads you buy.

So . . . you just went from an audience of everyone to an audience of a fraction the size. Not only are these folks hard to find, but they're picky as well.

Being first in the frozen pizza category was a good idea. Being first in pain relievers was an even better idea. Alas, they're both taken.

Let's consider yoga books for a second. The problem with books about how to do yoga is that there are too many of them.

A few years ago, when yoga books were scarce, all a publisher needed to be successful was a good yoga book. If people had a yoga problem, they'd visit the local bookstore, take a quick look at the three or four books available, and buy one.

Today, though, there are more than five hundred books on yoga. Nobody, no matter how motivated, takes the time to review all five hundred before buying a book on yoga. So if you've just written one, you've got a challenge ahead of you. Not only is there a huge amount of competition, but new books on yoga are useless to people who have already solved their yoga problem. All those folks who visited the store a few years ago and made yoga books so popular *are no longer shopping for yoga books!*

Here's the sad truth about marketing just about anything, whether it's a product or a service, whether it's marketed to consumers or to corporations:

> Most people can't buy your product. Either they don't have the money, they don't have the time, or they don't want it.

> If an audience doesn't have the money to buy what you're selling at the price you need to sell it for, you don't have a market.

> If an audience doesn't have the time to listen to and understand your pitch, you'll be treated as if you were invisible.

> And if an audience takes the time to hear your pitch but decides they don't want it . . . well, you're not going to get very far.

The world has changed. There are far more choices, but there is less and less time to sort them out.

This wasn't true just twenty years ago. Way back then, consumers had a lot more time and far fewer choices. Our disposable income had fewer ways to get squandered, so if a company came up with a really neat innovation (the cell phone, for example), we'd find a way to pay for it.

Years ago, our highly productive economy figured out how to satisfy almost everyone's needs. Then the game changed — it was all about satisfying our *wants*. The marketing community taught us (with plenty of TV advertising) to want more and more, and consumers did their best to keep up.

Among the people who *might* buy your product, most will never hear about it. There are so many alternatives now that people can no longer be easily reached by mass media. Busy consumers ignore unwanted messages, while your competition (which already has market share to defend) is willing to overspend to maintain that market share.

Worse still, people are getting harder to reach by permission media. Just because you have someone's email address or phone number doesn't mean they want to hear from you! And setting aside the spam issues, even when people *do* want to hear from you by phone or mail or email, they are less and less likely to take action. Your satisfied consumers value these messages less because those messages no longer solve their current problems. Companies have gotten better at understanding what satisfies their consumers (and presumably have gotten better at delivering it), so the bar keeps getting raised as to what product news you can possibly deliver that will add to that satisfaction. I wasn't being totally facetious when I quoted the former head of the U.S. Patent and Trademark Office. Almost everything we can realistically imagine that we need *has* been invented.

The last hurdle is that ideavirus networks are hard to

ignite in markets that are fairly satisfied. Because marketers have overwhelmed consumers with too much of everything, people are less likely to go out of their way to tell a friend about a product unless they're fairly optimistic that the friend will be glad to hear about it. When was the last time someone told you about a new pain reliever? It's a boring topic, and your friend is not going to waste your time. There's too much noise, and consumers are less eager than ever to add to it.

This is true not just for consumer products but also for business and industrial purchases. People who buy for businesses — whether it's advertising, parts, service, insurance, or real estate — just aren't as needy as they used to be. The folks who got there before you have a huge inertia advantage. If you want to grow your market share or launch something new, you have a significant challenge ahead.

Bottom line?

- All the obvious targets are gone, so people aren't likely to have easily solved problems.

- Consumers are hard to reach because they ignore you.

- Satisfied customers are less likely to tell their friends.

The old rules don't work so well any more. Marketing is dead. Long live marketing.

THE DEATH OF THE
TV-INDUSTRIAL COMPLEX

Remember the much-maligned "military-industrial complex"? The idea behind it was simple. The government spent money on weapons. Companies received tax dollars to build weapons. These companies hired labor. They paid taxes. The taxes were used to buy more weapons. A virtuous cycle was created: The government got bigger, employment went up, and it appeared that everyone was a winner.

The military-industrial complex was likely responsible for many of the world's ills, but it was undeniably a symbiotic system. As one half of it grew and prospered, so did the other.

Little noticed over the past fifty years was a very different symbiotic relationship, one that arguably created far more wealth (with large side effects) than the military-industrial complex did. I call it the *TV-industrial complex*. The reason we need to worry about it is that it's dying. We built a huge economic engine around the idea of this system, and now it's going away. The death of the complex is responsible for much of the turmoil at our companies today.

The system was simple. Find a large market niche that's growing and not yet dominated. Build a factory. Buy a lot of TV ads. The ads will lead to retail distribution and to sales. The sales will keep the factory busy and create profits.

Astute businesses then used all the profits to buy more ads. This led to more distribution and more factories. Soon the virtuous cycle was in place, and a large, profitable brand was built.

As the brand was built, it could command a higher price, generating larger profits and leaving more money for more TV ads. Consumers were trained to believe that "as seen on TV" was proof of product quality, so they looked for products on television. Non-advertised brands lost distribution and, ultimately, profits.

No, it's not rocket science, but that's partly why it worked so well. Big marketers with guts (like Procter & Gamble) were able to dominate entire categories by using this simple idea.

The old system worked for Revlon. Charles Revson was one of the first big TV advertisers, and advertising grew his company dramatically. Where did he spend his profits? On more TV ads.

In 1962, a smart ad agency hired Jay Ward, creator of Bullwinkle, and asked him to make a commercial. He invented Cap'n Crunch and came back with an animated commercial. Then, and only after that was done, did the cereal company go about actually making a cereal. Quaker knew that if they had a commercial, they could run enough ads to imprint the Cap'n into just about every kid in America. The cereal was secondary.

You could never afford to introduce Cap'n Crunch today, regardless of who made your commercial. Kids won't listen. Neither will adults.

Consumers were kids in the candy store; they had pockets filled with shiny money and they had a real desire to buy stuff. We shopped on TV and we shopped in stores. We were in a hurry and we wanted to fill our houses, our fridges, and our garages.

A quick look down this list of Procter & Gamble brands turns up significant proof of the presence of the TV-industrial complex. Is it possible to read the list without filling your head with images and jingles?

Bold, Bounce, Bounty, Cascade, Charmin, Cheer, Cover Girl, Crest, Dawn, Downy, Folgers, Head & Shoulders, Herbal Essences, Ivory, Max Factor, Miss Clairol, Mr. Clean, Nice 'n Easy, Noxzema, NyQuil, Oil of Olay, Old Spice, Pampers, Pepto-Bismol, Pringles, Safeguard, Scope, Secret, Tampax, Tide, Vicks, Vidal Sassoon, and Zest. Throw in particularly annoying product pitches like Wisk and Irish Spring, and the point is obvious. Advertising this stuff used to work. Really well.

It's hard for me to overstate the effectiveness of this system. Every time you buy a box of breakfast cereal, you're seeing the power of TV at work. Due to a commercial you likely saw thirty years ago, you're spending an extra dollar or two on a box of puffed wheat or sugared corn. Over your lifetime, that's thousands of dollars in cost premium for TV ads just for breakfast cereal.

Of course, it wasn't just supermarket brands. It was John Hancock and Merrill Lynch and Prudential. Archer Daniels Midland, Jeep, and Ronald Reagan as well. Big brands, big ideas, big impacts on our lives.

TV commercials are the most effective selling medium ever devised. A large part of the success of the American century is due to our companies' perfecting this medium and exploiting it to the hilt.

Our cars, our cigarettes, our clothes, our food — anything that was effectively advertised on TV was changed by the medium. Not only did marketers use television to promote their products, but television itself changed the way products were created and marketed. As a result, all of the marketing *P*s were adjusted to take advantage of the synergies between our factories and our ability to capture the attention of the audience.

Of course, it's not just TV that's fading. It's newspapers and magazines — any form of media interrupting any form of consumer activity. Individuals and businesses have ceased to pay attention.

The TV-industrial complex lasted a half-century — a long time. So long that the people who devised the strategies and ads that worked so well are gone. There's no one left at Philip Morris or General Foods who remembers what life was like before TV created the bureaucratic behemoths.

And that's the problem. The TV-industrial complex is hemorrhaging, and most marketers don't have a clue what to do about it. Every day, companies spend millions to re-create the glory days of the TV-industrial complex. And every day, they fail.

The old rule was this:

CREATE SAFE, ORDINARY PRODUCTS AND
COMBINE THEM WITH GREAT MARKETING.

The new rule is:

CREATE REMARKABLE PRODUCTS THAT
THE RIGHT PEOPLE SEEK OUT.

We can see the same thing in a simple chart:

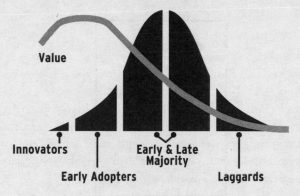

The marketer of yesterday valued the volume of people she could reach. The center of the black curve above was the goal. Mass marketing traditionally targets the early and late majority because this is the largest group. But in many markets, the **value** of a group isn't related to its size — a group's value is related to its influence. In this market, for example, the early adopters heavily influence the rest of the curve, so persuading them is worth far more than wasting ad dollars trying to persuade anyone else.

BEFORE AND AFTER

TV–INDUSTRIAL AGE	POST–TV AGE
AVERAGE PRODUCTS	REMARKABLE PRODUCTS
ADVERTISE TO ANYONE	ADVERTISE TO THE EARLY ADOPTER
FEAR OF FAILURE	FEAR OF FEAR
LONG CYCLES	SHORT CYCLES
SMALL CHANGES	BIG CHANGES

CONSIDER THE BEETLE

The ad that launched the Beetle to everyone.

The original VW Beetle was not as much of a counterculture car as you may remember. Its sales languished until some brilliant advertising saved it. On the basis of this great TV and print campaign, the car was profitable in the United States for more than fifteen years. The original Beetle is a poster child for the power of the TV-industrial complex.

In this case, it was the shape, not the ads, that worked.

The new Beetle, on the other hand, was a success because of the way it looked and the way it felt to drive. Good reviews, great word of mouth, and a distinctive shape that marketed it far and wide — these factors were responsible for the new Beetle's success. Every time the very round Beetle drove down a street filled with boxy SUVs, it was marketing itself.

After marketing the new Beetle for just three years, VW is now offering incentives, new designs, and other features to make the car exciting again. The Purple Cow works, but, alas, it doesn't last as long as good old TV domination did.

TV-INDUSTRIAL COMPLEX PRODUCTS

BARBIE, PRELL, HONEYWELL, UNITED AIRLINES, MCDONALD'S, MARLBORO, CAP'N CRUNCH, BATTLING TOPS, EXCEDRIN, THE ORIGINAL BEETLE

PURPLE COW PRODUCTS

STARBUCKS, MAGIC CARDS, DR. BRONNER'S, LINUX, JETBLUE, OUTBACK STEAKHOUSE, MOTEL 6, MP3, DR. BUKK, PROZAC, THE NEW BEETLE

WHAT WORKS?

One way to figure out a great theory is to look at what's working in the real world and figure out what the various successes have in common.

With marketing, though, it's puzzling. What could the Four Seasons and Motel 6 have in common? Other than the fact that both experienced extraordinary success and growth in the hotel field, they couldn't be more different. Or Wal-Mart and Neiman Marcus, both growing during the same decade. Or Nokia (changing its hardware every thirty days) and Nintendo (marketing the same Game Boy for fifteen years in a row).

It's like trying to drive by watching the rear-view mirror. Sure, those things worked, but do they help us predict what will work tomorrow?

What all of these companies have in common is that they have nothing in common. They are outliers. They're on the fringes. Super-fast or super-slow. Very exclusive or very cheap. Very big or very small.

The reason it's so hard to follow the leader is this: The leader is the leader because he did something remarkable. And that remarkable thing is now taken — it's no longer remarkable when you do it.

WHY *The Wall Street Journal*
ANNOYS ME SO MUCH

The *Journal* is the poster child for marketing old-think. Every day, more than a million dollars' worth of full-page ads run in this paper — testimony to traditional marketers' belief that the old ways are still valid.

A full-page ad in the *Journal* costs more than a house in Buffalo, New York. Page after page of dull gray ads, each pitching a dull product offering from a dull company.

If you took 90 percent of these ads and swapped the logos around, no one could tell. Switch one stock photo of a guy in a black derby hat with another stock photo of an earnest-looking pan-Asian smiling employee, and no one could tell.

One morning, with time to kill at a fine hotel, I interrupted a few people who were reading the *Journal* over breakfast. I waited until they had finished the first section, and then I asked them if they could name just two of the companies that had run full-page ads. Not one person could.

Then I took one of the ads, folded down the bottom with the logo, and asked the *Journal* readers which company ran the ad. No idea.

Finally, I asked them the million-dollar question (literally). Had they ever requested more information about a product because they'd seen a full-page ad in the *Journal*?

You can probably guess the answer.

It's not just TV that's broken. Just about all the ways marketers promote themselves (whether they sell to businesses or to consumers) are becoming less effective.

Here's the entire text of a full-page ad from a recent *Wall Street Journal*:

INTRODUCING KPMG CONSULTING'S NEW NAME AND ERA OF EMPOWERMENT

WE HAVE DONE MORE THAN JUST CHANGE OUR NAME. WE HAVE CHARTERED A NEW BEGINNING. AN ERA OF EMPOWERMENT. WHICH POSITIONS BEARINGPOINT-FORMERLY KPMG CONSULTING-READY TO ASSUME THE LEAD AS THE WORLD'S MOST INFLUENTIAL AND RESPECTED BUSINESS ADVISOR AND SYSTEMS INTEGRATOR. BUT WHILE WE HAVE CHANGED OUR NAME TO BEARINGPOINT, WHAT WE HAVE NOT CHANGED IS OUR MINDSET-THE DESIRE TO GET IT DONE. AND GET IT DONE RIGHT. OUR GOAL IS TO BE ON EVERYONE'S LIST. AT THE TOP, OF COURSE. WE WILL ACCOMPLISH THAT GOAL THE SAME WAY WE HAVE OPERATED FOR OVER 100 YEARS. ONE ON ONE. WITH PRACTICAL KNOW-HOW. WITH PASSION. DELIVERING TO OUR PRESENT AND FUTURE CLIENTS MORE THAN JUST CONSULTING. BY HELPING OUR CLIENTS ALIGN THEIR BUSINESS AND SYSTEMS TO ACHIEVE THEIR DESIRED GOALS. PROVIDING THE RIGHT INFORMATION TO EMPOWER THEIR BUSINESS. BECAUSE THE RIGHT INFORMATION BRINGS KNOWLEDGE. AND KNOWLEDGE IS POWER. SHARING IT IS EMPOWERMENT.

A committee wrote this ad. A committee approved it. No one will remember it; no one will point it out to a colleague. Advertising doesn't have to be this bad. It could be remarkable. It could help spread the word about a remarkable product.

Just because it's an ad doesn't mean it can't be remarkable. If the goal of the advertiser was to create a measurable impact — to create ads that actually got people to sit up, take notice, and tell their colleagues — the ads would be a lot better than they are today. But even that wouldn't be enough.

Awareness Is Not the Point

The marketing old guard is quick to defend the power of the TV commercial. They're delighted to point out the great success stories of years past, and to happily articulate why only TV can get the awareness needed to launch a new product or maintain an existing one.

Yet Sergio Zyman, the marketing guru who was there for most of Coca-Cola's rebirth, points out that two of the most popular TV commercials of all time—"I'd like to teach the world to sing" and "Mean Joe Greene"—sold not one more bottle of Coke. They entertained and got attention, but they translated into no incremental revenue. He jokes that the commercial should have been, "I'd like to teach the world to drink."

In Sergio's words, "Kmart has plenty of awareness. So what?"

THE WILL AND THE WAY

I don't think there's a shortage of remarkable ideas. I think your business has plenty of great opportunities to do great things. Nope, what's missing isn't the ideas. It's the will to execute them.

My goal in *Purple Cow* is to make it clear that it's safer to be risky — to fortify your desire to do truly amazing things. Once you see that the old ways have nowhere to go but down, it becomes even more imperative to create things worth talking about.

One of the best excuses your colleagues will come up with, though, is that they *don't* have the ability to find the great idea, or if they do, they don't know how to distinguish the great idea from the lousy ideas. This book isn't long enough for me to outline all of the spectacularly successful brainstorming, ideation, and creativity techniques that are used by companies around the world. What I can do, though, is highlight the takeaway ideas, the specific things you can do tomorrow to start on your way to the Purple Cow. If you've got the will, you'll find the way.

The symbol ◉ will mark my top takeaway points, spread throughout the book.

CASE STUDY: GOING UP?

Elevators certainly aren't a typical consumer product. They can easily cost more than a million dollars, they generally get installed when a building is first constructed, and they're not much use unless the building is more than three or four stories tall.

How, then, does an elevator company compete? Until recently, selling involved a lot of golf, dinners, and long-term relationships with key purchasing agents at major real estate developers. No doubt this continues, but Otis Elevator Company has radically changed the game by developing a Purple Cow.

Walk into the offices of Cap Gemini in Times Square, and you're faced with a fascinating solution. The problem? Every elevator ride is basically a local. The elevator stops five, ten, fifteen times on the way to your floor. This is a hassle for you, but it's a huge, expensive problem for the building. While your elevator is busy stopping at every floor, the folks in the lobby are getting more and more frustrated. The building needs more elevators, but there's no money to buy them and nowhere to put them.

Otis's insight? When you approach the elevators, you key in your floor on a centralized control panel. In return, the panel tells you which elevator will take you to your floor.

With this simple pre-sort, Otis has managed to turn every elevator into an express. Your elevator takes you immediately to the twelfth floor and races back to the lobby. This means that buildings can be taller, they need fewer elevators for a given number of people, the wait is shorter, and the building can use precious space for people, not for elevators. A huge win, implemented at remarkably low cost.

Is there a significant real estate developer in the world who is unaware of this breakthrough? Not likely. And it doesn't really matter how many ads or how many lunches the competition sponsors; Otis now gets the benefit of the doubt.

◉ **Instead of trying to use your technology and expertise to make a better product for your users' standard behavior, experiment with inviting the users to change their behavior to make the product work dramatically better.**

CASE STUDY: WHAT SHOULD TIDE DO?

Tide is arguably the best laundry detergent in history. Every year, Procter & Gamble invests millions of dollars and pays a top-flight team of chemists to push the performance of Tide further and further.

Is that the right thing to do?

Tide succeeded early on because of a mixture of good TV ads, very good distribution, and a great product. As the TV-industrial complex crumbled, though, the ads mattered less and less. Now, with the ascension of Wal-Mart, the distribution is more crucial than ever. One chain of stores accounts for a third of Tide's sales. Without Wal-Mart, Tide is dead.

So what should P&G do? Are they likely to come up with a true innovation, a remarkable breakthrough that even casual detergent buyers notice? Or are the incremental improvements largely a carryover from a different time, a time when people actually cared about their laundry?

Orthodox Purple Cow thinking would have P&G take the profits while they're still there. Cut research spending, raise the price as much as is practical, and put the incremental profits into the creation of ever more radical and interesting new products. If the current R&D isn't likely to generate a noteworthy payoff, what's the point?

◉ **If a product's future is unlikely to be remarkable — if you can't imagine a future in which people are once again fascinated by your product — it's time to realize that the game has changed. Instead of investing in a dying product, take profits and reinvest them in building something new.**

GETTING IN

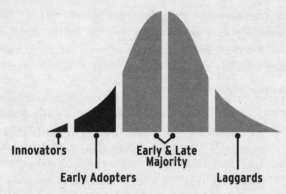

Innovators

Early Adopters

Early & Late Majority

Laggards

Only the risk-taking, idea-spreading people on the left part of the curve are willing to listen to you.

If we look at the idea diffusion curve, we see that the bulk of product sales come *after* a product has been adopted by the consumers willing to take a chance on something new. Those early adopters create an environment where the early and late majority feel safe buying the new item. The sales that matter don't come until the left part of the curve is completely sold.

The big insight here, though, is that the vast majority of the curve ignores you. Every time. People in the early and late majority listen to their experienced peers but are going to ignore you. It is so tempting to skip the left and go for the juicy center. But that doesn't work anymore.

Regardless of industry, successful new products and services follow this familiar pattern after they are introduced. First they are purchased by the innovators. These are the people in a given market who like having something first. They may not even need the product; they just want it. Innovators are the folks who sit in the front row at a fashion show in Paris, go to Internet World, and read edgy trade journals.

Right next to innovators on Moore's curve are the early adopters. (No, they're not early *adapters* — that would be just about the opposite, wouldn't it?) Early adopters are the folks who can actually benefit from using a new product and who are eager to maintain their edge over the rest of the population by seeking out new products and services. It might be a new investment device (zero-coupon bonds, say) or even a new TV show, but in any meaningful market, this audience is both sizable and willing to spend money.

Trailing after the early adopters are the early and late majority. These consumers don't necessarily yearn for a new product or service that can benefit them, but if enough of their peers try it and talk about it, these followers are likely to come along as well.

It's essential to realize two things about this big and profitable group. First, these people are really good at ignoring you. They have problems that they find far more significant than the ones your product solves, and they're just not willing to invest the time to listen to you.

Second, they often don't even listen to the innovators on the left part of the curve. The early and late majority want protocols and systems and safety that new products rarely offer. Countless products never manage to get far enough along the curve to reach these folks. And if they're not even going to listen to their friends, why should they listen to you?

Finally, the laggards complete the curve, getting around to buying a cassette deck when the rest of us have moved on to CDs. If anything, these people are the adapters. They don't use something new until it's so old that what they used to use is obsolete, impractical, or not even available any longer.

No one is going to eagerly adapt to your product. The vast majority of consumers are happy. Stuck. Sold on what they've got. They're not looking for a replacement, and they don't like adapting to anything new. You don't have the power to force them to. The only chance you have is to sell to people who like change, who like new stuff, who are actively looking for what it is you sell. Then you hope that the idea spreads, moving from the early adopters to the rest of the curve. After the early adopters embrace what you're selling, *they* are the ones who will sell it to the early majority — not you. And they will sell it poorly. (Moore talks at length about moving through the rest of the curve. I highly recommend his book.)

You must design a product that is remarkable enough to attract the early adopters — but is flexible enough and attractive enough that those adopters will have an easy time spreading the idea to the rest of the curve.

Digital cameras have been attractively priced for about five years. At the beginning, only gadget-heads and computer geeks bought them. Digital cameras were a little tricky to use, and the quality wasn't great. Over time, the camera manufacturers obsessed about fixing both problems and were rewarded with dramatically increased sales. Digital cameras are well on their way to replacing film cameras. This shift was not caused by great ad campaigns from the camera companies. Instead, it is the direct result of early adopters successfully selling the cameras to their friends.

Digital cameras spread because they offer convenience and price advantages over film cameras. Better still, these advantages are obvious, easy to talk about, easy to demonstrate, and just begging to be brought up every time an early adopter sees a laggard pull out a film camera.

Being remarkable in the right way helps you in two ways.

First, it makes it far easier to attract the left side of the curve. And second, it makes it easier for these early adopters to persuasively sell their peers on the rest of the curve.

IDEAS THAT SPREAD, WIN

A brand (or a new product offering) is nothing more than an idea. *Ideas that spread are more likely to succeed than those that don't.* I call ideas that spread, *ideaviruses*.

Sneezers are the key spreading agents of an ideavirus. These are the experts who tell all their colleagues or friends or admirers about a new product or service on which they are a perceived authority. Sneezers are the ones who launch and maintain ideaviruses. Innovators or early adopters may be the first to buy your product, but if they're not sneezers as well, they won't spread your idea. They're selfish in their use of a new idea, or they don't have the credibility to spread it to others. Either way, they're a dead end when it comes to spreading an idea.

Every market has a few sneezers. They're often the early adopters, but not always. Finding and seducing these sneezers is the essential step in creating an ideavirus.

So how do you create an idea that spreads? Don't try to make a product for everybody, because that is a product for nobody. The everybody products are all taken. The sneezers in these huge markets have too many choices and are too satisfied for it to be likely that you will capture their interest.

The way you break through to the mainstream is to target a niche instead of a huge market. With a niche, you can segment off a chunk of the mainstream, and create an ideavirus so focused that it overwhelms that small slice of the market that really and truly will respond to what you sell. The early adopters in this market niche are more eager to hear what you have to say. The sneezers in this market niche are more likely to talk about your product. And best of all, the market is small enough that a few sneezers can get you to the critical mass you need to create an ideavirus.

Then, if you're good and you're lucky, that innovation will diffuse. After it dominates the original niche, it will migrate to the masses.

◉ It's not an accident that some products catch on and some don't. When an ideavirus occurs, it's often because all the viral pieces work together. How smooth and easy is it to spread your idea? How often will people sneeze it to their friends? How tightly knit is the group you're targeting – do they talk much? Do they believe each other? How reputable are the people most likely to promote your idea? How persistent is it – is it a fad that has to spread fast before it dies, or will the idea have legs (and thus you can invest in spreading it over time)?

Put all of your new product developments through this analysis, and you'll discover which ones are most likely to catch on. Those are the products and ideas worth launching.

THE BIG MISUNDERSTANDING

The problem with the books I mentioned earlier — *Crossing the Chasm* and *The Tipping Point* and *Unleashing the Ideavirus* — is that many marketers got exactly the wrong idea.

Marketers who read these books often conclude that these ideas are gimmicks that work every once in a while, or that the ideas sound organic and automatic and natural. An idea *becomes* an ideavirus. It crosses the chasm. It tips. All these consumers seem to be busy doing your job, spreading your idea from one person to another, so you can sit back and wait for success to happen.

At the same time, the poor schnooks at Procter & Gamble and Nike and Colgate-Palmolive are spending $4 billion a year on advertising.

Guess what? Both groups are wrong. While ideaviruses are occasionally the result of luck (consider the Macarena, say, or the Pet Rock), the vast majority of product success stories are engineered from the first day to be successful.

Marketing in a post-TV world is no longer about making a product attractive or interesting or pretty or funny *after* it's designed and built — it's about designing the thing to be virus-worthy in the first place. Products that are engineered to cross the chasm — with built-in safety nets for wary consumers — are way more likely to succeed than are products not engineered that way. Services that are *worth* talking about *get* talked about.

The hard work and big money you used to spend on frequent purchases of print and TV advertising now move to repeated engineering expenses and product failures. If anything, marketing is more time-consuming and expensive than it used to be. You're just spending the money earlier in the process (and repeating the process more often). This is worth highlighting: The Purple Cow is not a cheap shortcut. It is, however, your best (perhaps *only*) strategy for growth.

The Purple Cow isn't cheap, but it works. We need to understand that investing in the Cow is even smarter than buying a Super Bowl ad.

WHO'S LISTENING?

I'm guilty of a little hyperbole. With all the hand wringing over the death of the TV-industrial complex and the predictions of the demise of all mass media, it's easy to jump to the conclusion that ads don't work at all — that every consumer avoids and ignores all of them.

Of course, this isn't true. Ads do work — not as well as they used to, and perhaps not cost-effectively, but they do attract attention and generate sales. Targeted ads are far more cost-effective, yet most advertising and marketing efforts are completely untargeted. They are hurricanes, whipping through a marketplace horizontally, touching everyone in the same way, regardless of who they are and what they want. There's a huge amount of waste here, so much that it's easy to assert that advertising isn't working. Yes, sometimes this hurricane allows you to skip the painstaking work of moving from the left to the right. Sometimes the entire market needs something, knows they need it, and are willing to listen. The key word here, though, is *sometimes*.

Sometimes is pretty rare — so rare that it's wasteful. It's wasteful because the vast majority of ads reach people who are not in the market for what's being sold, or who aren't likely to tell their friends and peers about what they've learned.

But a very different kind of ad does work. Why? What is it about some ads and some products that makes them successful, while others fail? Why, for example, do the little text-only ads on Google perform so well while the flashy, full-page, annoying banners on Yahoo! do so poorly?

We have to start with another look at the power in the marketing equation. In the old days, marketers *targeted* consumers. Smart ad folks worked hard to make sure their ad was appropriate for the target market and that the ad ran in media that would reach that market. Implicit in the idea of targeting, though, is the conceit that it was up to the marketers to decide who would pay attention and when.

Today, of course, the opposite is true. It's the consumers who choose. They choose whether you are listened to or ignored. How do they decide? Are some consumers more likely than others to listen? What separates the listeners from the others?

The big secret of Google ads is that they are both contextually relevant and presented to the type of person who's likely to act on them. You see a Google "ad" just moments after you've typed in a search term for that very item! Compare this to a loud, unwelcome interruption of a less-focused consumer, and the difference is clear.

At any given moment, in any given market, some people are all ears. They want to hear from you. They look through the Yellow Pages, subscribe to trade magazines, and visit Web sites looking for more information. Some of these people will eventually buy; some are just looking.

So here comes the big idea:

IT IS USELESS TO ADVERTISE TO ANYONE

(EXCEPT INTERESTED SNEEZERS WITH INFLUENCE).

You need to do this advertising when these consumers are actually looking for help, and in a place where they'll find you. Of course, advertising to one interested person is a good idea, but the real win occurs when the person who's listening is a sneezer likely to tell her friends and colleagues.

Obviously, the chances you have to advertise to this select audience are rare. The rest of the time, you need to be investing in the Purple Cow. Products, services and techniques so useful, interesting, outrageous, and noteworthy that the market will want to listen to what you have to say. No, in fact, you must develop products, services, and techniques that the market will actually *seek out*.

Cheating

- *JetBlue Airways is cheating.* Their low-cost structure, underused airports, and young, non-union staff give them an unfair advantage.
- *Starbucks is cheating.* The coffee bar phenomenon was invented by them, and now whenever we think coffee, we think Starbucks.
- *Vanguard is cheating.* Their low-cost index funds make it impossible for a full-service broker to compete.
- *Amazon.com is cheating.* Their free shipping and huge selection give them an unfair advantage over the neighborhood store.
- *Google is cheating.* They learned from the mistakes of the first-generation portals and they don't carry the baggage of their peers.
- *Wendy's is cheating.* Their flexibility allows them to introduce half a dozen salad-based entrees, capturing a big chunk of the adult market.
- *Ducati is cheating.* Because they don't have to make motorcycles for the entire market, they can specialize in high-profit, amazing bikes, which sell out every year.
- *HBO is cheating.* Because they have to program original shows only one night a week, HBO can focus and invest and cream the networks.

None of these companies are using the old-fashioned advertising-based techniques to win. To their entrenched (but nervous) competitors, these companies appear to be cheating because they're not playing by the rules.

Why aren't you cheating?

WHO CARES?

You can't make people listen. But you can figure out who's likely to be listening when you talk, and then invent the right combination of *P*s to overwhelm them with the rightness of your offer.

Even if someone is listening, your offering of "a little bit cheaper," "a little bit better," or "a little bit easier" is just a waste of time. The influential sneezers, the people with a problem to solve — they're open to hearing your story only if it's truly remarkable; otherwise, you're invisible.

The "Who's listening?" question drives not just the success of individual products, but also the status of entire markets. Consider classical music for a second.

The classical music industry is now officially moribund. The big labels are hurting. Orchestras are seeing recording money dry up. There are virtually no commercially important new works being written or recorded.

Why?

Because no one is listening.

The influential sneezers already have all the music they're ever going to buy. Everything old that was worth recording *has* been recorded — and quite well, thank you. So the sneezers have stopped looking.

Because the sneezers have stopped looking, all of those folks farther down the curve, who seek their advice or listen to the radio stations, are busy buying cut-rate $8 versions of the classics. There's no money there for the record companies and the orchestras. Because listeners have stopped looking, composers are turning to film scores or lawn care as a way to make a living. There's an attention blockade, and no player in the music business has enough money to change the dynamic. Music marketers can't buy enough ads or reach enough sneezers to spread the word about interesting new music. So the entire market stops.

The insight here is *not* that the music industry ought to figure out a better way to solve this problem. They don't need a better form of advertising. The insight might be that there *isn't* a better way. The Naxos music label (they're the guys who sell the $8 CDs) is doing great. Why? Because they organized the product-marketing in all its forms — around the idea that sneezers wanted good, cheap versions of the music they already knew. Naxos was right. The market stopped listening. Naxos won.

Sony's classical label can't compete because they're not organized at the product level or the promotion level to win at that game. So they whither.

When faced with a market in which no one is listening, the smartest plan is usually to leave. Plan B is to have the insight and guts to go after a series of Purple Cows, to launch a product/service/promotional offering that somehow gets (the right) people to listen.

Not All Customers Are the Same

Michael Schrage writes about a large bank that discovered that 10 percent of their customers were using their online banking service *every day*, while the remainder were using it about once a month. At first glance, a consultant would argue that the bank should stop spending so much on the service, as it was appealing to only the innovators and some early adopters. Further digging, however, showed that this group also accounted for about 70 percent of the bank's deposits.

It's easy to look at the idea diffusion curve and decide that the juicy, profitable, wonderful place to be is right in the center, where all the people are. However, that's rarely true. Often, the valuable slices are located to one side or the other. What this bank might realize is that by focusing on these innovative customers, the bank may be able to bring in even more highly profitable risk-seeking customers, leaving the slow and declining sector to seek other (less profitable) banks.

⊚ **Differentiate your customers. Find the group that's most profitable. Find the group that's most likely to sneeze. Figure out how to develop/advertise/reward either group. Ignore the rest. Your ads (and your products!) shouldn't cater to the masses. Your ads (and products) should cater to the customers you'd choose if you could choose your customers.**

THE LAW OF LARGE NUMBERS

The magic of mass media and the Web is all tied up in the large numbers: 20 million people watching *The Sopranos*; 100 million watching the Super Bowl; a billion watching the Oscars; 3 million people using KaZaA at the same time, all the time; 120 million registered Yahoo! users. The numbers are compelling.

What if just one out of a thousand Oscar viewers tried your product? What if one member of every family in China sent you a nickel?

The problem with large numbers is that they're almost always accompanied by fractions with huge denominators. If you reach 100 million people, but only .000001 percent of the audience buys your product, well, you've just sold exactly one unit.

Years ago, when I first predicted the demise of the banner ad as we know it, people laughed at me. At the time, banner ads were selling for a CPM of $100. (CPM is the cost per thousand ad impressions.) That means you'd pay $100 for a thousand banners.

What advertisers who measured (the vast minority) soon realized was that every time they bought a thousand banners, they got exactly zero clicks. The banners had a hit rate of less than .000001 percent. The law of large numbers was at work.

Today, you can buy banner ads for less than a dollar a thousand. A 99 percent drop. I did a deal with one site in which I bought 300 million banner ads for a total cost of $600. The funny thing is that I lost money on the deal. Those 300 million banner ads (that's more than one banner impression for every single person in the United States) ended up selling less than $500 worth of merchandise.

As consumers get better and better at ignoring mass media, mass media stops working. Sure, there are always gimmicks that work (animated online pages or product tie-ins with reality TV shows come to mind), but the vast majority of ordinary advertising is victim to this unrepealable law.

SoundScan is a neat company with a fascinating product. Working with retailers and record companies, SoundScan knows exactly how many copies of every released album are sold, every week, in the entire country.

What's surprising is how horribly so many records do. In 2002, the *New York Times* reported that of the more than 6,000 albums distributed by the major labels, only 112 albums sold more than 500,000 copies last year. Many, many titles don't sell even *one* copy some weeks. What does it take to find a stranger, reach that stranger, teach that stranger, and then get that stranger to walk into a store and buy what you're selling? It's too hard.

In almost every market measured, the "leading brand" has a huge advantage over the others. Whether it's word processors, fashion magazines, Web sites, or hairdressers, a lot of benefits go to the brands that win. Often a lesser brand has no chance at all. There may be a lot of consumers out there, but they're busy consumers, and it's just easier to go with the winner. (Of course, this is true only until the "winner" stops being interesting — and then, whether it's cars, beer, or magazines, a new leader emerges.)

CASE STUDY: CHIP CONLEY

My friend and colleague Chip Conley runs more than a dozen hotels in San Francisco. His first hotel, the Phoenix, is in one of the worst neighborhoods downtown.

Chip got the hotel (it's really a motel) for next to nothing. He knew that it wasn't a hotel for everybody. In fact, no matter what he did to the Phoenix, hardly anyone would choose to stay there.

Which is fine. Because "hardly anyone" can be quite enough if you've got a hotel with just a few dozen rooms. Chip redesigned the place. He painted it funky colors. Put hip style magazines in all the rooms. Had a cutting-edge artist paint the inside of the pool, and invited up-and-coming rock-and-roll stars to stay at the place.

Within months, the plan worked. By intentionally ignoring the mass market, Chip created something remarkable: a rock-and-roll motel in the center of San Francisco. People looking for it found it.

◉ **Make a list of competitors who are not trying to be everything to everyone. Are they outperforming you? If you could pick one underserved niche to target (and to dominate), what would it be? Why not launch a product to compete with your own — a product that does nothing but appeal to this market?**

THE PROBLEM WITH THE COW

. . . is actually the problem with fear.

If being a Purple Cow is such an easy, effective way to break through the clutter, why doesn't everyone do it? Why is it so hard to be Purple?

Some folks would like you to believe that there are too few great ideas or that their product or their industry or their company can't support a great idea. This, of course, is nonsense.

The Cow is so rare because people are afraid.

If you're remarkable, it's likely that some people won't like you. That's part of the definition of remarkable. Nobody gets unanimous praise — ever. The best the timid can hope for is to be unnoticed. Criticism comes to those who stand out.

Where did you learn how to fail? If you're like most Americans, you learned in first grade. That's when you started figuring out that the safe thing to do was to fit in. The safe thing to do was to color inside the lines, don't ask too many questions in class, and whatever you do, be sure your homework assignment fits on the supplied piece of card stock.

We run our schools like factories. We line kids up in straight rows, put them in batches (called grades), and work very hard to make sure there are no defective parts. Nobody standing out, falling behind, running ahead, making a ruckus.

Playing it safe. Following the rules. Those seem like the best ways to avoid failure. And in school, they may very well be. Alas, these rules set a pattern for most people (like your boss?), and that pattern is awfully dangerous. These are the rules that ultimately lead to failure.

In a crowded marketplace, fitting in is failing. In a busy marketplace, not standing out is the same as being invisible.

Jon Spoelstra, in *Marketing Outrageously*, points out the catch-22 of the Purple Cow. If times are tough, your peers and your boss may very well say that you can't afford to be remarkable. After all, we have to conserve, to play it safe; we don't have the money to make a mistake. In good times, however, those same people will tell you to relax, take it easy; we can afford to be conservative, to play it safe.

The good news is that the prevailing wisdom makes your job even easier. Since just about everyone else is petrified of the Cow, you can be remarkable with even less effort. If successful new products are the ones that stand out, and most people desire not to stand out, you're set!

So it seems that we face two choices: to be invisible, anonymous, uncriticized, and safe, or to take a chance at greatness, uniqueness, and the Cow.

According to the *New York Times*, a fourteen-block stretch of Amsterdam Avenue in New York contains about seventy-four restaurants. What's most noticeable about these restaurants is how boring they are. Sure, they offer cuisine from twenty or thirty cultures, and the food is occasionally quite good, but there are precious few remarkable places here. The restaurants are just plain dull compared to the few amazing restaurants in New York.

Why? Simple. After spending all that money and all that time opening a restaurant, the entrepreneur is in no mood to take yet another risk. A restaurant that's boring won't attract much criticism. If it's just like the others, no one will go out of their way to bad-mouth it. Ray's Pizza is just plain average. You won't get sick, but you won't grin with pleasure, either. It's just another New York pizza place. As a result, the owner makes a living, rarely having to worry about a bad review or offending anyone.

We've been raised with a false belief: We mistakenly believe that criticism leads to failure. From the time we get to school, we're taught that being noticed is almost always bad. It gets us sent to the principal's office, not to Harvard.

Nobody says, "Yeah, I'd like to set myself up for some serious criticism!" And yet . . . the only way to be remarkable is to do just that.

Several decades ago, when Andrew Weil went to Harvard Medical School, the curriculum was much the same as it is today. The focus was on being the best doctor you could be, not on challenging the medical establishment.

Weil took a different path than his peers did. Today, his books have sold millions of copies. He gets the satisfaction of knowing that his writing, speaking, and clinics have helped hundreds of thousands of people. And he's really, really rich. All because he did something that most of his classmates would view as reckless and risky. The fascinating thing is that while the vast majority of those doctors are overworked, tired, and frustrated at the system they helped create and work every day to maintain, Andrew Weil is having a blast. *Being safe is risky.*

We often respond to our aversion to criticism by hiding, avoiding the negative feedback, and thus (ironically) guaranteeing that we won't succeed! If the only way to cut through is to be remarkable, and the only way to avoid criticism is to be boring and safe, well, that's quite a choice, isn't it?

You do not equal the project. Criticism of the project is *not* criticism of you. The fact that we need to be reminded of this points to how unprepared we are for the era of the Cow. It's people who have projects that are *never* criticized who ultimately fail.

Will you do some things wrong in your career and be

justly criticized for being unprepared, sloppy, or thought-less? Sure you will. But these errors have nothing at all to do with the ups and downs you'll experience as a result of being associated with the Purple Cow. When you launch a clunker, the criticism of the failure will be real, but it won't be about you—it'll be about the idea. The greatest artists, playwrights, car designers, composers, advertising art directors, authors, and chefs have all had significant flops—it's part of what makes their successful work great.

Cadillac's new CTS, in my humble opinion, is perhaps the ugliest car ever produced outside the Soviet bloc. Cadillac has been roundly criticized in car magazines, at dealerships, and on countless online bulletin boards. Guess what? These cars are selling. Fast. It's a rebirth for a tired brand, the biggest success Cadillac has had in decades. What difference does it make that the "official" critics don't like the car? The people who are buying it love it.

On the list of most profitable movies of 2002, right next to *Spider-Man* and *Goldmember*, is a surprise: *My Big Fat Greek Wedding*. Criticized by Hollywood for being too low-key (and by the independents for not being original or edgy), this $3 million sleeper succeeded for exactly those two reasons. A cheap, feel-good date movie was just exceptional enough to stand out—and the market grabbed it.

Almost forty years ago, Bob Dylan, one of my favorite Purple Cows, appeared at the Newport Folk Festival. He was practically burned in effigy. The act of "going electric" was viewed as treason. He had abandoned the cause, they said, and they were angry. "They" were also wrong.

In 2001, billionaire Mike Bloomberg ran for mayor of New York. He was criticized, shunned, booed, and worst of all, dismissed as a dilettante. But he won. Go figure.

After the failure of the Apple Newton (wonderfully satirized in *Doonesbury* as a bizarre technological dead end), the folks who invented the Palm Pilot had their work cut out for them. Early models didn't work. Early co-ventures failed. They blew a trademark fight and lost their name to a Japanese pen company. The easy and smart thing to do would have been to give up and go do good work at some R&D lab. But the founders persisted, continuing to make their device single-minded (when conventional wisdom demanded multi-purpose devices) and cheap (when conventional wisdom demanded expensive high-tech introductions). The founders were exceptional, and they won.

Only when Palm tried to play it safe did they start to stumble. Three years in a row of incremental feature creep has cost them market share and profit.

Compare these successes to the Buick. The Buick is a boring car. It's been boring for almost fifty years. Few people aspire to own a Buick. The Buick isn't easy to criticize, but it's also not very successful, is it?

Drugstore.com is another boring company. They have a boring Web site, selling boring stuff. (When was the last time someone got excited about Braun launching a new toothbrush?) Is there much to criticize about the way they do business? Not really. But there's no Cow there. As a result, very few new customers go out of their way to do business with them.

So how are you going to predict which ideas are going to backfire and which are guaranteed to be worth the hard work they take to launch? The short answer: You can't.

Hey, if it was easy to become a rock star, everyone would do it!

You can't know if your Purple Cow is guaranteed to work. You can't know if it's remarkable enough or too risky. That's the point. It's the very unpredictability of the outcome that makes it work.

The lesson is simple —boring always leads to failure.*
Boring is always the most risky strategy. Smart businesspeople realize this, and they work to minimize (but not
eliminate) the risk from the process. They know that
sometimes it's not going to work, but they accept the fact
that that's okay.

*Except, of course, when being boring is, in and of itself, remarkable.

FOLLOW THE LEADER

Why do birds fly in formation? Because the birds that follow the leader have an easier flight. The leader breaks the wind resistance, and the following birds can fly far more efficiently. Without the triangle formation, Canadian geese would never have enough energy to make it to the end of their long migration.

A lot of risk-averse businesspeople believe that they can follow a similar strategy. They think they can wait until a leader demonstrates a breakthrough idea, and then rush to copy it, enjoying the break in wind resistance from the leader.

If you watch the flock closely, though, you'll notice that the flock doesn't really fly in formation. Every few minutes, one of the birds from the back of the flock will break away, fly to the front, and take over, giving the previous leader a chance to move to the back and take a break.

The problem with people who would avoid a remarkable career is that they never end up as the leader. They decide to work for a big company, intentionally functioning as an anonymous drone, staying way back to avoid risk and criticism. If they make a mistake and choose the wrong bird to follow, they lose. When a big company lays off ten thousand people, most of those people probably don't deserve to get fired. They were doing what they were told, staying within the boundaries, and following instructions. Alas, they picked the wrong lead bird.

Even if you find a flock that's pretty safe, in our turbulent world, it's harder and harder to stay in formation, and we often find ourselves scurrying to find a new flock. The ability to lead is thus even more important because when your flock fades away, there may be no other flock handy.

This is true not just for individual careers, of course. Companies have the same trouble. They follow an industry leader that stumbles. Or they launch a thousand imitations of their first breakthrough product—never realizing that the market is drying up.

For years, the record business has been dominated by a few major players, and they work hard to follow each other's lead. The labels have similar pricing, merchant policies, contracts, and packaging. Each label avoids criticism by sticking with the pack.

But when the market changes — when technology reshuffles the deck — the record labels are all in trouble. With no practice leading, no practice trying the unknown, they're trapped, panicked, and in serious trouble. Their trade organization, the RIAA, is spending millions of dollars lobbying Congress to get legislation to keep the world just the way it is. In the long run, of course, they'll fail. You can't keep the world the way it is, even if you buy the influence of Congress.

The lesson of the Cow is worth repeating: *Safe is risky.*

◉ **What tactics does your firm use that involve following the leader? What if you abandoned them and did something very different instead? If you acknowledge that you'll never catch up by being the same, make a list of ways you can catch up by being different.**

Case Study: The Aeron Chair

Before Herman Miller, desk chairs were invisible. A desk chair got spec'ed and acquired by the Purchasing or Human Resources department gnomes, and unless you were the CEO, you didn't get much say in where you sat. And you might not have even noticed the difference between one cushy desk chair and another.

The buyers of desk chairs were searching for a safe and easy choice. The manufacturers listened carefully to the buyers and made safe and easy choices. This was a dull market with dull results.

When Herman Miller introduced the $750 (gasp) Aeron chair in 1994, they took a radical risk. They launched a chair that looked different, worked differently, and cost a bunch. It was a Purple Cow. Everyone who saw it wanted to sit in it, and everyone who sat in it wanted to talk about it. The designers at Herman Miller knew that the chair was expensive enough that it wasn't a safe purchase for the ordinary purchasing agent. They also knew that it was quite likely that they wouldn't sell many chairs at all.

Herman Miller got it right, though. Sitting in the Aeron chair sent a message about what you did and who you were, and buying the chairs for your company sent a message as well. Soon after the Aeron came out, Seth Goldstein—founder of SiteSpecific (the first online direct-marketing ad agency)—took his very first venture-capital check and went straight out to buy more than a dozen Aeron chairs. That got him on the front page of the *Wall Street Journal*.

This isn't a case of inventing some gimmick to create an example of the much fabled but rarely achieved viral marketing. Instead, it's about putting the marketing investment into the product instead of into the media. Millions of Aeron chairs have been sold since its introduction in 1994, and the chair is now in the permanent collection of the Museum of Modern Art.

"The best design solves problems, but if you can weld that to the cool factor, then you have a home run," says Mark Schurman of Herman Miller. Another way of saying that Herman Miller realized that making a safe chair was the single riskiest thing they could do.

PROJECTIONS, PROFITS, AND
THE PURPLE COW

Mass marketing demands mass products. And mass products beg for mass marketing.

This equation leads to a dangerous catch-22, one with
two parts.

Part One: Boring Products. Companies that are built
around mass marketing develop their products accordingly. These companies round the edges, smooth out the dif-
ferentiating features, and try to make products that are
bland enough to work for the masses. These companies
make spicy food less spicy, and they make insanely great
service a little less great (and a little cheaper). They push
everything—from the price to the performance — to the
center of the market. They listen to the merchandisers at
Kmart and Wal-Mart or the purchasing agents at Johnson
& Johnson and make products that will appeal to everybody.

After all, if you're going to launch a huge ad campaign
by direct mail or in trade magazines or in daily newspapers
or on television, you want your ads to have the maximum
possible appeal. What's the point of advertising to everyone
a product that doesn't appeal to everyone? By following this
misguided logic, marketers ensure that their products have
the minimum possible chance of success.

Remember, those ads reach two kinds of viewers:

- The highly coveted innovators and adopters who will
  be bored by this mass-marketed product and decide
  to ignore it.

- The early and late majority who are unlikely to listen
  to an ad for any new product, and are unlikely to
  buy it if they do.

By targeting the center of the market and designing the product accordingly, these marketers waste their marketing dollars. Exhibit A: The dozens of consumer-focused dot-com companies who wasted more than a billion (a billion!) dollars advertising watered-down products to the mass market. Your grocery store is also a very public graveyard for mediocre products designed for the masses.

As we've already seen, the only way an idea reaches the bulk of the market is to move from left to right. You can no longer reach everyone at once. And if you don't grab the attention and enthusiasm of the sneezers, your product withers.

Part Two: Scary Budgets. In order to launch a product for the masses, you need to spend big. It's not unusual to spend a million dollars to launch something local, and spend a hundred times that to do an effective national rollout. For most of the three hundred major movies launched by Hollywood every year, the studios spend more than $20 million on marketing for *each movie.*

The problem with a scary budget is that you have to make the ads work, and quickly. If you don't break through the clutter, capture imagination and attention, get retailers excited and stocking your product, and get the factory unloading its inventory, well, it's over. You've wasted your shot; you don't get a second chance, and the product is considered dead.

The front-loading of the budget does two things to your product:

- It means you get very few chances to launch new products because each one is so expensive. Thus, you won't make risky bets, and you'll be even more likely to introduce boring, me-too products.

• It doesn't give you a chance to ride through the idea diffusion curve. It takes a while to reach the sneezers, who take a while to reach the rest of the population. But your front-loaded budget means that by the time the bulk of the population hears about what you've done, you've burned out the retailers, destroyed your inventory, or, worst of all, driven your startup company into bankruptcy.

Dozens of astonishingly great products were introduced during the dot-com boom. Alas, most of them never had a chance to diffuse. For example, a weatherproof package receptacle that only you and the UPS man knew the combination for. Or a tiny electronic gizmo that told you which bars, clubs, and restaurants in your town were hot and what was playing. Or a Web site where you could easily give feedback to big companies—and get your problems fixed.

In each case, a fledgling company spent most of its capital on mass marketing. Marketing that came too soon and disappeared before the idea could spread.

Compare this to the success of just about every movie that has surprised Hollywood over the past decade. When a *Blair Witch* or a *Greek Wedding* comes along, it doesn't get launched with a huge marketing budget. The filmmakers wisely focus on making a remarkable movie instead. So a few innovators (the folks who go to see every movie, just about) stumble onto the film, and the word starts to spread.

It seems obvious, yet just about every product aimed at a large audience (consumer and industrial) falls into this trap.

◎ **What would happen if you gave the marketing budget for your next three products to the designers? Could you afford a world-class architect/designer/sculptor/director/author?**

Case Study: The Best Baker in the World

Lionel Poilane's dad was a French baker, and he inherited the family bakery when he was a young man. Rather than sitting still and tending to the fires, though, Lionel became obsessed with remarkable.

He did extensive research, interviewing more than eight thousand French bakers about their techniques. He pioneered the use of organic flour in France. He refused to bake baguettes, pointing out that they were fairly tasteless and very un-French (they're a fairly recent import from Vienna). He acquired the largest collection of bread cookbooks in the world—and studied them.

His sourdough bread is made with just flour, water, starter, and sea salt, and it's baked in a wood-fired oven. Poilane refused to hire bakers — he told me they had too many bad habits to unlearn—and instead hired young men who were willing to apprentice with him for years.

At first, the French establishment rejected his products, considering them too daring and different. But the overwhelming quality of the loaves and Poilane's desire to do it right finally won them over.

Virtually every fancy restaurant in Paris now serves Poilane bread. People come from all over the world to wait in line in front of his tiny shop on Rue de Cherche Midi to buy a huge loaf of sourdough bread — or more likely, several loaves. The company he founded now ships loaves all over the world, turning handmade bread into a global product, one worth talking about.

Last year, Lionel sold more than $10 million worth of bread.

MASS MARKETERS HATE TO MEASURE

Direct marketers, of course, realize that measurement is the key to success. Figure out what works, and do it more!

Mass marketers have always resisted this temptation. When my old company approached the head of one of the largest magazine publishers in the world and pitched a technology that would allow advertisers to track who saw their ads and responded to them, he was aghast. He realized that this sort of data could kill his business. He knew that his clients didn't want the data because then their jobs would get a lot more complex.

Measurement means admitting what's broken so you can fix it. Mass-media advertising, whether it's on TV or in print, is all about emotion and craft, not about fixing mistakes. One reason the Internet ad boomlet faded so fast is that it forced advertisers to measure—and to admit what was going wrong.

Well, creators of the Purple Cow must measure as well. Every product, every interaction, every policy is either working (persuading sneezers and spreading the word) or not. Companies that measure will quickly optimize their offerings and make them more virus-worthy.

As it becomes easier to monitor informal consumer networks, the winners will be companies that figure out what's working fastest—and do it more (and figure out what's not working—and kill it).

Zara, a fast-growing retailer in Europe, changes its clothing line every three or four weeks. By carefully watching what's working and what's not, they can evolve their lineup far faster than the competition can ever hope to.

⊙ **What could you measure? What would that cost? How fast could you get the results? If you can afford it, try it. "If you measure it, it will improve."**

Case Study: Logitech

How did Logitech become the fastest-growing technology company in America? Their mouses (mice?), trackballs, and input devices aren't the best examples of cutting-edge technology coming out of Silicon Valley, certainly. And the lack of cutting-edge technology is a key part of their success.

Logitech succeeds because management understands that they are in the fashion business. The guts of their devices don't change often—but the functionality and style change constantly. Management isn't busy trying to figure out how to innovate a better chip. They are, on the other hand, working frantically to create a better user experience.

For the frequent user, the impact of a cooler, better, easier-to-use input device is profound— so profound that many users are happy to proselytize to their peers. More sneezing of a Purple Cow. Logitech doesn't crave more advertising. They crave more remarkable products. That's what their customers want to buy.

WHO WINS IN THE WORLD OF THE COW

It's fairly obvious who the big losers are — giant brands with big factories and quarterly targets, organizations with significant corporate inertia and low thresholds for perceived risks. Once addicted to the cycle of the TV-industrial complex, these companies have built hierarchies and systems that make it awfully difficult to be remarkable.

The obvious winners are the mid-sized and smaller companies looking to increase market share. These are the companies that have nothing to lose, but more important, they realize that they have a lot to gain by changing the rules of the game. Of course, there are big companies that get it and have the guts to take the less risky path, just as there are small companies that are stuck with their current products and strategies.

As I write this, the number-one song in Germany, France, Italy, Spain, and a dozen other countries in Europe is about ketchup. The song is called "Ketchup," and it is by two sisters you never heard of. The number-two movie in America is a low-budget animated movie in which talking vegetables act out Bible stories. Neither thing is the sort of product you'd expect from a lumbering media behemoth.

Sam Adams beer was remarkable, and it captured a huge slice of business from Budweiser. Hard Manufacturing's $3,000 Doernbecher crib opened up an entire segment of the hospital crib market. The electric piano let Yamaha steal an increasingly larger share of the traditional-piano segment away from the entrenched market leaders. Vanguard's remarkably low-cost mutual funds continue to whale away at Fidelity's market dominance. BIC lost tons of market share to Japanese competitors when they developed pens that were remarkably fun to write with, just as BIC stole the market away from fountain pens a generation or two earlier.

Case Study: A New Kind of Kiwi

The last time New Zealand successfully introduced a fruit to North America (which in itself is a cool postmodern idea), it was the gooseberry. They renamed it the "kiwi," introduced it to yuppies, foodies, and upscale supermarkets, and watched it take off.

Today, diffusing an idea about a new fruit is much more difficult. How then to launch a new kiwi, one that's golden with an edible peel?

Zespri, the only company that knows how to grow the new kiwi, aimed at a niche—Latino foodies. The new kiwi has a lot in common with mangoes and papayas but is different enough to be remarkable. By targeting upscale Latino groceries, Zespri found underserved produce buyers who had both the time and the inclination to try something that was new and exclusive.

So, without advertising at all, Zespri gets the fruit in front of an audience of risk-taking sneezers. If Zespri is aggressive in doing in-store tasting, they've got an excellent chance of working their way through the Latino community and then eventually crossing over to the rest of the mass market. Last year, Zespri managed to sell more than $100 million worth of golden kiwi fruit, but unless you're Latino, you've probably never even seen it.

THE BENEFITS OF BEING THE COW

So it's an interesting paradox. As the world gets more turbulent, more and more people seek safety. They want to eliminate as much risk as they can from their businesses and their careers.

And most of the people mistakenly believe that the way to do that is to play it safe. To hide. So fewer and fewer people work to create a new Purple Cow.

At the same time, the marketplace is getting faster and more fluid. Yes, we're too busy to pay attention, but a portion of the population is more restless than ever. Some people are happy to switch their long distance service, their airline, their accounting firm — whatever it takes to get an edge. If the bank teller annoys you, well, there's another bank right down the street. So while fewer people attempt to become the Cow, the rewards for being remarkable continue to *increase!* At work is the ability of a small portion of eager experimenters to influence the rest of us.

As the ability to be remarkable continues to demonstrate its awesome value in the marketplace, the rewards that follow the Purple Cow increase.

Whether you develop a new insurance policy, record a hit record, or write a best-selling, groundbreaking book, the money, prestige, power, and satisfaction that follow are extraordinary. In exchange for taking the risk—the risk of failure or ridicule or unfulfilled dreams — the creator of the Purple Cow gets a huge upside when she gets it right.

Even better, these benefits have a half-life. You don't have to be remarkable all the time to enjoy the upside. Starbucks was remarkable a few years ago. Now they're boring. But that first burst of innovation and insight has allowed them to grow to thousands of stores around the world. Starbucks is unlikely to keep up their blistering growth rate unless they find another Cow, but the benefits that came to them were huge. Compare this growth in assets to Maxwell House. Ten years ago, all the brand value in coffee resided with them, not with Starbucks. But Maxwell House played it safe (they thought), and now they remain stuck with not much more than they had a decade ago.

In just about every industry and just about every career, the creator of the Purple Cow receives huge benefits. Star football players get long-term contracts. The authors of a fluke best-seller like *The Nanny Diaries* managed to sign a million-dollar deal for a sequel, even though the new book can't possibly be as successful. A hot agency easily signs up new clients on the basis of their success with their old clients. Same reason.

Once you've managed to create something truly remarkable, the challenge is to do two things simultaneously:

- Milk the Cow for everything it's worth. Figure out how to extend it and profit from it for as long as possible.

- Create an environment where you are likely to invent a new Purple Cow in time to replace the first one when its benefits inevitably trail off.

Of course, these are contradictory goals. The creator of a Purple Cow enjoys the profits, the accolades, and the feeling of omniscience that comes with a success. None of those outcomes accompany a failed attempt at a new Cow. Thus, the tempting thing to do is to coast. Take profits. Fail to reinvest. Take no chances because those "chances" seem to be opportunities to blow the very benefits you worked so hard to earn.

Palm, Yahoo!, AOL, Marriott, Marvel Comics . . . the

list goes on and on. Each company had a breakthrough, built an empire around it, and then failed to take another risk.

It used to be easy to coast for a long time after a few remarkable successes. Disney coasted for decades. Milton Berle did, too. It's too easy to decide to sit out the next round, rationalizing that you're spending the time and energy to build on what you've got instead of investing in the future.

CASE STUDY: THE ITALIAN BUTCHER

There are literally thousands of butchers in Italy, but only one of them is famous (and only one of them is rich). Dario Cecchini has been profiled in magazine articles and guidebooks. His 250-year-old butcher shop in Panzano almost always has a crowd. People come from all over the world to visit his shop — to hear him quote Dante and rhapsodize about the Fiorentina beefsteak. When the European Economic Union banned the sale of steak with the bones left in (because of the fear of mad cow disease*), Dario Cecchini held a mock funeral and buried a steak in front of his store — complete with casket.

Is his meat that much better? Probably not. But by turning the process of buying meat into an intellectual and political exercise, Dario has figured out more than one way to make money from a cow — this time, a purple one.

*Alas, Purple Cow disease is not contagious.

Wall Street and the Cow

Current market conditions notwithstanding, what's the secret to every entrepreneur's dream, the successful IPO? The companies that successfully went public during the Net boom (and those that will follow when the market comes back) had one thing in common — they'd created a Purple Cow and proved it.

Whether it was insanely popular chat sites or beta versions of database software that key early adopters raved about, each company had a story to tell the Street. So investors bought in.

Then just about every company forgot the lesson of the Cow. Instead of taking the money and using it to create a series of innovations that could lead to the next Cow (at a higher, bigger level), these companies took profits. The companies streamlined and mechanized and milked their Cow. Alas, very few markets are stable enough and fast — or long-growing enough to allow a public company to thrive for very long. Their days of 20 percent annual growth are probably gone forever.

THE OPPOSITE OF "REMARKABLE"

is "very good."

Ideas that are remarkable are much more likely to spread than ideas that aren't. Yet so few brave people make remarkable stuff. Why? I think it's because they think that the opposite of "remarkable" is "bad" or "mediocre" or "poorly done." Thus, if they make something very good, they confuse it with being virus-worthy. Yet this is not a discussion about quality at all.

If you travel on an airline and they get you there safely, you don't tell anyone. That's what's supposed to happen. What makes it remarkable is if it's horrible beyond belief *or* if the service is so unexpected (they were an hour early! they comped my ticket because I was cute! they served flaming crêpes suzette in first class!) that you need to share it.

Factories set quality requirements and try to meet them. That's boring. Very good is an everyday occurrence and hardly worth mentioning.

◉ **Are you making very good stuff? How fast can you stop?**

THE PEARL IN THE BOTTLE

Remember Prell? All of us boomers certainly can envision the clear bottle of shampoo filled with green liquid . . . and the pearl slowly drifting downward. This image was omnipresent in the advertising for Prell.

The commercial never made it clear precisely what a pearl had to do with shampoo or why we wanted the pearl to move slowly. What is beyond dispute is that TV commercials made this rather ordinary shampoo a significant success.

Where do you find a Purple Cow in the cosmetics business? After all, almost all shampoos are the same. More often than not, it's an extraneous exotic ingredient or fancy packaging that people notice, not the effectiveness of the potion.

Compare the inexorable decline of Prell (the TV commercials stopped working) with the gradual ascent of Dr. Bronner's.

Dr. Bronner's does no advertising at all, yet their product continues to grow in sales and market share. If it's not

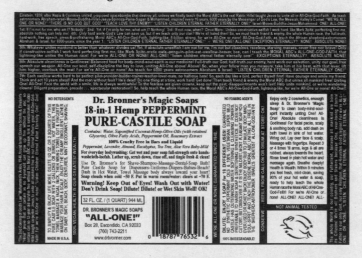

because of a better product, then why? Because of the incredible packaging. The packaging is very much part of the experience of using the product.

Most people discover this extraordinary product at a friend's house. Brushing your teeth in the guest bathroom, with nothing much better to do than snoop, you inevitably start reading the thousands of words inscribed all around the bottle. "Balanced food for mind-body-spirit is our medicine."

Not only is it unique, but the uniqueness is aimed at a specific audience, one in which the early adopters are more than happy to proselytize to their friends.

Dr. Bronner's is a truly remarkable shampoo as shampoos go. It's worth noticing, worth talking about, and for many people, worth buying. In a world without (effective) ads, it has an unfair advantage against anything the big guys can develop.

◉ **Buy a bottle of Dr. Bronner's. Now, working with your factory and your designers, Bronnify a variation of one of your products.**

THE PARODY PARADOX

J. Peterman is back. His oblong white catalog—filled with lengthy descriptions of Mata Hari, duster coats from cowboys on the prairie, and irreplaceable white silk scarves—was solidly entrenched in the zeitgeist a decade ago. The writing was so over the top that a fictional J. Peterman even became a character on *Seinfeld*.

A tiny ad in The New Yorker *launched this duster coat and the idiosyncratic voice behind the J. Peterman catalog. It was so remarkable that it spread, and as it spread, it became ripe for parody.*

Imagine for a second the same thing happening to L.L. Bean or Lands' End. Inconceivable. Those catalogs are safe and steady and boring. The original J. Peterman catalog, on the other hand, was so ridiculous that it was delightful to parody. We feel the same way about Martha Stewart's obsessive calendar in the front of her magazine or the two "cheeseburgah" guys at that diner in Chicago, as parodied by John Belushi and Dan Aykroyd.

In each of these cases, the very uniqueness that led to a parody results in a huge increase in attention, in sales, and in profits. If you can show up in a parody, it means you've got something unique, something worth poking fun at. It means there's a Purple Cow at work. The paradox is this: The same word of mouth that can make your product a huge hit can also lead to someone's snickering at you.

Most companies are so afraid of offending or appearing ridiculous that they steer far away from any path that might lead them to this result. They make boring products because they don't want to be interesting. When a committee gets involved, each well-meaning participant sands off the rough edges, speaking up for how their constituency might not like the product. The result is something boring and safe.

◉ **How could you modify your product or service so that you'd show up on the next episode of** *Saturday Night Live* **or in a spoof of your industry's trade journal?**

SEVENTY-TWO PEARL JAM ALBUMS

The music business is all about interrupting jaundiced strangers with news about ever more similar acts, all trying to break into the Top 40. Ninety-seven percent of all records lose money because this model is fundamentally broken.

Of course, in 1962 this was a brilliant strategy. People were starved for great new music. Retailers wanted more titles to stock, radio stations wanted more acts, and consumers wanted bigger collections. Advertising (in the form of radio payola or retail spiffs) was quite effective. No longer.

Virtually all breakthrough acts in the music business now are the result of blind luck (and a little talent). A band (brand?) captures the interest of a small group of sneezers, who tell their friends, and suddenly they've got a hit. Rather than accepting this, though, the music industry tries to manufacture hits the old way.

Except for Pearl Jam. They seem to get it. They broke through. They worked hard (and got lucky), recorded some hits, and became headliners. Then, instead of insisting that they could do it again and again and again, they rallied their core audience and built a very different system.

If you're a Pearl Jam fan, you know that from 2001 through 2002, the band released seventy-two live albums, all available on their Web site. They're not trying to interrupt strangers; they're selling to the converted. Pearl Jam knows that once they have permission to talk to someone, it's much easier to make a sale. They know that the cost of selling an album to this audience is relatively minuscule, and they've turned a profit on all seventy-two albums. The big win on top of this income stream occurs when some of this core audience is so delighted by this bounty of great products that they take the time to indoctrinate their friends. Thus, the Pearl Jam universe grows. Big fans bring in new fans, and old fans stick around because they're catered to. There's very little leakage because the band keeps the existing customer base satisfied with remarkable products.

◉ **Do you have the email addresses of the 20 percent of your customer base that loves what you do? If not, start getting them. If you do, what could you make for these customers that would be super-special? Visit www.sethgodin.com and you can sign up for my list and see what happens.**

CASE STUDY: CURAD

When Curad wanted to challenge the Band-Aid brand for the market for adhesive bandages, most people thought Curad was crazy. Band-Aid was a household institution, a name so well known it was practically generic. And the product was terrific. What could Curad hope to accomplish?

Curad developed a Purple Cow—bandages with characters printed on them.

Kids, the prime consumers of small bandages, loved them. So did parents who wanted to make the boo-boos get better even faster! And of course, when the first kid with Curads wore them to school, every other kid wanted them, too.

It didn't take very long at all for Curad to grab a chunk of market share away from the market leader.

◉ **Could you make a collectible version of your product?**

SIT THERE, DON'T JUST DO SOMETHING

Marketing departments often feel a need to justify their existence. If last year's slogan feels old, they'll spend a million dollars to invent and propagate a new one. If retail sales are down, marketers will hire a consultant to freshen up their store look.

All too often, these marketing efforts are the result of a compromise. Either a budget compromise ("We don't have enough money to launch a new product; let's launch a new slogan") or a product compromise ("That will offend our existing customer base; let's do something less radical"). Almost without exception, these compromises are worse than doing nothing.

If you do nothing, at least you're not going to short-circuit your existing consumer networks by loading them up with a lot of indefensible junk. When you do nothing, your sneezers can still trumpet the original cool stuff that made you popular in the first place. The constant "refreshing" of your line with ever more mediocre messaging and products just makes it harder for your few remaining fans to spread the word.

Ben & Jerry's avoided temptation for years. If they didn't have a super-cool flavor or a great promotional idea, they did nothing. Yes to free ice cream once a year at every scoop shop, but *no* to 5 percent off any pint this week at your local store. McIntosh, a leading manufacturer of high-end stereo equipment, has done the same thing. Instead of launching a few amplifiers a year, McIntosh launches a few a decade. This tactic may not satisfy the junior people in the Engineering department (fewer cool projects), but it helps build the legend and work the products through the adoption curve.

Doing nothing is not as good as doing something (great). But marketing just to keep busy is worse than nothing at all.

Seth Godin

◉ What would happen if you took one or two seasons off from the new-product grind and reintroduced wonderful classics instead? What sort of amazing thing could you offer in the first season you came back (with rested designers)?

CASE STUDY: UNITED STATES
POSTAL SERVICE

Very few organizations have as timid an audience as the
United States Postal Service. Dominated by conservative
big customers, the Postal Service has a very hard time
innovating. The big direct marketers are successful
because they've figured out how to thrive under the current system, and they're in no mood to see that system
change. Most individuals are in no hurry to change their
mailing habits, either.

The majority of new policy initiatives at the Postal
Service are either ignored or met with nothing but dis-
dain. But ZIP+4 was a huge success. Within a few years, the
Postal Service diffused a new idea, causing a change in billions of address records in thousands of databases. How?

First, it was a game-changing innovation. ZIP+4 makes
it far easier for marketers to target neighborhoods, and
much faster and easier to deliver the mail. The product
was a Purple Cow, completely changing the way customers
and the Postal Service deal with bulk mail. ZIP+4 offered
both dramatically increased speed in delivery and a signif-
icantly lower cost for bulk mailers. These benefits made it
worth the time it took mailers to pay attention. The cost of
ignoring the innovation would be felt immediately on the
bottom line.

Second, the Postal Service wisely singled out a few early
adopters. These were individuals in organizations that were
technically savvy and were extremely sensitive to both pricing
and speed issues. These early adopters were also in a position
to sneeze the benefits to other, less astute, mailers.

The lesson here is simple: The more intransigent your
market, the more crowded the marketplace, the busier

your customers, the more you need the Purple Cow. Half-measures will fail. Overhauling the product with dramatic improvements in things the right customers care about, on the other hand, can have a huge payoff.

IN SEARCH OF *Otaku*

The Japanese have invented some truly useful words. One of them is *otaku*. *Otaku* describes something that's more than a hobby but a little less than an obsession. *Otaku* is the overwhelming desire that gets someone to drive across town to try a new ramen-noodle shop that got a great review. *Otaku* is the desire to find out everything about Lionel's new digital locomotive—and to tell your fellow hobbyists about it.

People read *Fast Company* because they have an *otaku* about business. They visit trade shows to stay on the cutting edge —not just to help their company survive, but because they like that edge. *Otaku*, it turns out, is at the heart of the Purple Cow phenomenon.

As we saw earlier, your company can't thrive just by fulfilling basic needs. You must somehow connect with passionate early adopters and get those adopters to spread the word through the curve. And that's where *otaku* comes in.

Consumers with *otaku* are the sneezers you seek. They're the ones who will take the time to learn about your product, take the risk to try your product, and take their friends' time to tell them about it. The flash of insight is that some markets have more *otaku*-stricken consumers than others. The task of the remarkable marketer is to identify these markets and focus on them to the exclusion of lesser markets —regardless of relative size.

There's a healthy vein of hot-sauce *otaku* in the United States, for example. Chili-heads in search of ever hotter elixirs, the biggest possible burn, have made the production of these insane sauces into a real business. Examples? Dave's Insanity, Blair's After Death Hot Sauce, Mad Dog 357, Pain 100%, Mad Dog Inferno, Boar's Breath, Sweet Mama Jamma's Mojo Juice, Melinda's XXXX, Mad Cat, Lost in

Boiling Lake, Satan's Revenge, and the always popular Trailer Trash. At the same time that dozens of entrepreneurs have created successful hot-sauce businesses with no advertising, no one has made any impact selling mustard.

Arguably, there are more people who enjoy mustard than people who enjoy brain-scorching 25,000-Scoville-unit hot sauce. Yet hot sauce is a business and mustard isn't. Why? Because very few people will order mustard by mail or request a different brand at a restaurant. They don't have the *otaku*.

Smart businesses target markets where there's already *otaku*.

◎ **Go to a science fiction convention. These are pretty odd folks. Do you appeal to an audience as wacky and wonderful as this one? How could you create one? (Jeep did. So did *Fast Company* and the Longaberger basket company. There are similar groups in the investing community, the market for operating systems, and the market for million-dollar stereo systems. Products differ, but sneezers and early adopters stay the same.)**

CASE STUDY: HOW DUTCH BOY STIRRED UP THE PAINT BUSINESS

It's so simple it's scary. They changed the can.

Paint cans are heavy, hard to carry, hard to close, hard to open, hard to pour from, and no fun. Yet they've been around for a long time, and most people assumed there had to be a reason.

Dutch Boy realized that there was no reason. They also realized that the can was an integral part of the product— people don't buy paint; they buy painted walls, and the can makes the painting process much easier.

Dutch Boy used this insight and introduced an easier-to-carry, easier-to-pour-from, easier-to-close paint jug. Sales went way up — no surprise when you think about it. Not only did the new packaging increase sales, but it also got Dutch Boy paint more distribution (at a higher retail price!).

A few obvious changes in the can meant a huge surge in sales for Dutch Boy. The obvious question: Why did it take so long?

This is marketing done right. Marketing where the marketer changes the product, not the ads.

SETH GODIN

◉ **Where does your product end and marketing hype begin? The Dutch Boy can is clearly product, not hype. Can you redefine what you sell in a similar way?**

CASE STUDY: KRISPY KREME

There are two kinds of people — those who have heard the legend of Krispy Kreme donuts and assume that everyone knows it, and those who live somewhere where the donut dynasty hasn't yet shown up.

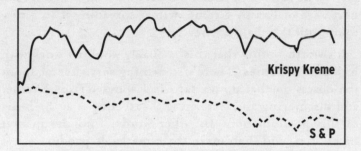

Since the day of their IPO, Krispy Kreme has totally demolished all expectations, drastically outperforming just about every other stock. Why? Krispy Kreme understands how to manage the Cow.

Krispy Kreme makes a good donut. No doubt about it. But is it a donut worth driving an hour for? Apparently, donut maniacs believe it is. And this very remarkable fact is at the core of Krispy Kreme's success.

When Krispy Kreme opens in a new town, they begin by giving away thousands of donuts. Of course, the people most likely to show up for a free hot donut are those who have heard the legend of Krispy Kreme and are delighted that they're finally in town.

These sneezers are quick to tell their friends, sell their friends, even drag their friends to a store. And that's where the second phase kicks in. Krispy Kreme is obsessed with dominating the donut conversation. Once they've opened their flagship stores in an area, they rush to do deals with gas stations, coffee shops, and delis. The goal? To make it easy for someone to stumble onto the product. They start with people who will drive twenty miles, and finish with people too lazy to cross the street.

If the product stays remarkable (and Krispy Kreme is betting millions that it will), then some of those lazy people will be converted to the donut *otaku*. They will start the next wave of Krispy Kreme mania, spreading it in a new town until the chain arrives.

It's worth noting that this probably wouldn't work with bagels or brownies. There's something very visceral about the obsession that donut fans feel about Krispy Kreme, and discovering and leveraging that feeling is at the heart of this phenomenon. In other words, find the market niche first, and then make the remarkable product — not the other way around.

THE PROCESS AND THE PLAN

So is there a foolproof way to create a Purple Cow every time? Is there a secret formula, a ritual, an incantation that you can use to increase creativity at the same time you stay firmly grounded in reality?

Of course not.

There is no plan. The eventual slowdown of almost every Purple Cow company indicates that there's no rule book listing things that always produce. That's one reason that seeing the insight of the Cow is so difficult. Looking in our rear-view mirror, we can always say, "Of course that worked." By definition, a genuine Purple Cow is something that was remarkable in just the right way. When we take our eyes off the rear-view mirror, though, creating a Purple Cow suddenly gets a lot more difficult.

If you were looking to this book for a plan, I'm sorry to tell you that I don't have one. I do, however, have a process. A system that has no given tactics but is as good as any.

The system is pretty simple: Go for the edges. Challenge yourself and your team to describe what those edges are (not that you'd actually go there), and then test which edge is most likely to deliver the marketing and financial results you seek.

By reviewing every other P — your pricing, your packaging, and so forth—you sketch out where your edges are . . . and where your competition is. Without understanding this landscape, you can't go to the next step and figure out which innovation you can support.

Would it be remarkable if your spa offered all its services for free? Sure, but without a financial model that supports that, it's not clear that you'd last very long. JetBlue figured out how to get way over to the edge of both service and pricing — with a business that was also profitable. Archie McPhee did it in retail with their product selection. Starbucks determined how to redefine what a cup of coffee meant (in a way very different from the way JetBlue delivered their innovation).

It's not the tactics or the plan that joins the Purple Cow products together. It's the process organizations use to discover (intentionally or accidentally) the fringes that make their products remarkable.

THE POWER OF A SLOGAN

Slogans used to be important because you could put them in TV commercials and get your message across in just a few seconds. Today, that same conciseness is important but for a different reason.

A slogan that accurately conveys the essence of your Purple Cow is a script. A script for the sneezer to use when she talks with her friends. The slogan reminds the user, "Here's why it's worth recommending us; here's why your friends and colleagues will be glad you told them about us." And best of all, the script guarantees that the word of mouth is passed on properly — that the prospect is coming to you for the right reason.

Tiffany's blue box is a slogan without words. It stands for elegance and packaging and quality and "price is no object." Every time someone gives a gift in the Tiffany's box, she's spreading the word. Just like the Hooters name and logo or the funky hipness of Apple's industrial design, each company has managed to position itself in a coherent way and make it easy to spread the word to others.

The Leaning Tower of Pisa sees millions of visitors every year. It's exactly as advertised. It's a leaning tower. There's nothing to complicate the message. There's no "also," "and," or "plus." It's just the leaning tower in the middle of a lawn. Put a picture on a T-shirt, and the message is easily sent and received. The purity of the message makes it even more remarkable. It's easy to tell someone about the Leaning Tower. Much harder to tell them about the Pantheon in Rome. So, even though the Pantheon is beautiful, breathtaking, and important, it sees I percent of the crowds that the harder-to-get-to Tower in Pisa gets.

Every one of these examples highlights the fact that this is not marketing done *to* a product. The marketing *is* the product, and vice versa. No smart marketer transformed Hooters or the Leaning Tower of Pisa. The marketing is built right in.

◉ **Do you have a slogan or positioning statement or remarkable boast that's actually true? Is it consistent? Is it worth passing on?**

Case Study: The Häagen-Dazs in Bronxville

The nearest Häagen-Dazs is just like all the other ice cream shops you've been to. They've got cones, bars, and frozen yogurt. Only two things are different about a Häagen-Dazs shop: it's cleaner and a lot better run. How come?

Well, sitting on the counter is a stack of large business cards. The card lists the name and office phone number of the owner of the store. And then the card says, "If you have any comments at all about the store, please call me at home." And it lists the owner's home phone number.

People who visit, notice. People who work there realize that the customers are noticing. It's all very remarkable. Stand in the store for twenty minutes, and you're sure to hear one customer mention the cards to another. If every store owner did this, it probably wouldn't work. But because it's so unusual, the customers take notice and the staff is on alert.

◎ **If you're in an intangibles business, your business card is a big part of what you sell. What if everyone in your company had to carry a second business card? Something that actually sold them (and you). Something remarkable. Imagine if Milton Glaser or Chip Kidd designed something worth passing on. So go do it!**

Sell What People Are Buying (and Talking About!)

A few years ago, after yet another unsuccessful sales call, I realized the blindingly obvious: It's a lot easier to sell something that people are already in the mood to buy.

As obvious as this may seem, most marketers don't get it. For example, Butterball has invented a new use for turkey (and its brand) and has introduced fast-baking pot pies, now in your grocer's freezer. The problem is that the audience for this very retro food isn't necessarily in the market for a brand-new way to feed their family. What's worse, Butterball is introducing the product with TV commercials running on the Food Channel.

I'm trying hard to imagine Butterball's target customer. The Food Channel viewer is busy watching a cooking show, and here's an insipid, soft-focus commercial for a glorified TV dinner. How many viewers will even watch the commercial? Of those watching, how many will respond in the way Butterball hopes? Worse, how many will tell a friend about this great new meal?

On the list of people who are baking a frozen comfort food for dinner, there are few risk-taking early adopters. And among those adopters, very few, it seems to me, are going to look to the Food Channel for the answer to their "What's new?" problem.

Consumers with needs are the ones most likely to respond to your solutions. Whether your prospect is an industrial bearings buyer at Ford or an overworked househusband in Tucson, you need to figure out who's buying, and then solve their problem. Butterball's product is unremarkable. It doesn't solve anyone's problem except for Butterball's. Butterball's advertising and media choices make it worse.

The alternative is to start with a problem that you can solve for your customer (who realizes he has a problem!). Then, once you've come up with a solution that is so remarkable that the early adopters among this population will gleefully respond, you've got to promote it in a medium where those most likely to sneeze are actually paying attention. Altoids' campaign is a great example. They realized that young adults who weren't taking up smoking were looking for something to do with their fingers and their mouths while at work — and Hershey's bars weren't going to cut it.

By advertising in urban centers with cutting-edge imagery and slogans, Altoids spoke directly to this market about a need that customers didn't even know they had. By creating a tin that just begged to be shared, Altoids made it easy for early adopters to sneeze the product to the rest of the market. The result: one of the most profitable candy introductions ever.

The Problem with Compromise

The old saying is right: "A camel is a horse designed by a committee." If the goal of marketing is to create a Purple Cow, and the nature of the Cow is to be extreme in some attribute, it's inevitable that compromise can only diminish your chances of success.

Compromise is about sanding down the rough edges to gain buy-in from other constituencies. Vanilla is a compromise ice cream flavor, while habanero pecan is not. While there may be just a few people who are unwilling to eat vanilla ice cream, there are legions of people who are allergic to nuts, sensitive to spicy food, or just plain uninterested in eating a challenging scoop of ice cream. The safe compromise choice for a kid's birthday party is the vanilla. But vanilla is boring. You can't build a fast-growing company around vanilla.

In almost every market, the boring slot is filled. The product designed to appeal to the largest possible audience already exists, and displacing it is awfully difficult. Difficult because the very innocuousness of the market-leading product is its greatest asset. How can you market yourself as "more bland than the leading brand"? The real growth comes with products that annoy, offend, don't appeal, are too expensive, too cheap, too heavy, too complicated, too simple — too something. (Of course, they're too *too* for some people, but just perfect for others.)

Bootstrapping entrepreneurs often upend existing industries because the dominant players in an industry are the last places you'll find empowered mavericks. The market-leading companies may owe their dominance to the Purple Cow they marketed years and years ago, but today, they're all about compromising themselves to continued profitability. The seeds of their destruction lie in their dependence on being in the middle.

◉ **If someone in your organization is charged with creating a new Purple Cow,** *leave them alone!* **Don't use internal reviews and usability testing to figure out if the new product is as good as what you've got now. Instead, pick the right maverick and get out of the way.**

CASE STUDY: MOTOROLA AND NOKIA

Guess what? Cell phones are now boring. Just about everyone who needs a phone now has one. Most people who want a phone have one, too. The companies that built this revolution now have a problem: What next?

What do they have to put into a phone to get people to notice it? Is it possible to make a remarkable phone anymore? What both companies have discovered is that smaller phones no longer create excitement, so they needed something new. Nokia just introduced a $21,000 cell phone called Vertu—designed to be not just a phone but a remarkable piece of jewelry as well. At the same time, both companies are working on disposable phones that they hope will be remarkably cheap.

In a totally different direction, both companies are scrambling to market phones that send photographs. Of course, both the sender and the recipient have to have the right kind of phone, but that might be a good thing.

The sad truth, though, is that it may be quite a while before the market generates the attention it did five years ago. The Purple Cow has left the room, and there's not a lot the cell phone companies can do about it.

The Magic Cycle of the Cow

Does our chaotic world guarantee that your efforts to bring new ideas to the marketplace are guaranteed to be chaotic as well? Are we doomed to randomly invent stuff for an ever-changing roster of potential consumers?

I don't think so. The reason is that many consumers don't change their roles very often. Sneezers love to sneeze. They're often open to hearing from marketers who are pretty reliable in their track record of creating Purple Cows. But cocooned, scared consumers (in business or at home) keep their ears closed virtually all the time. The cautious consumers are stuck in their habitual mode, just like the sneezers are.

But it's the sneezers we care about, and we can leverage the fact that if we respect them, they'll listen.

The four steps, then, are these:

1. Get permission from people you impressed the first time. Not permission to spam them or sell them leftovers or squeeze extra margins from them. Permission to alert them the next time you might have another Cow.

2. Work with the sneezers in that audience to make it easier for them to help your idea cross the chasm. Give them the tools (and the story) they'll need to sell your idea to a wider audience.

3. Once you've crossed the line from remarkable to profitable business, let a different team milk it. Productize your services, servicize your products, let a thousand variations bloom. But don't believe your own press releases. This is the inevitable downward slide to commodity. Milk it for all it's worth, and fast.

4. Reinvest. Do it again. With a vengeance. Launch another Purple Cow (to the same audience). Fail and fail and fail again. Assume that what was remarkable last time won't be remarkable this time.

This may not be nearly as predictable or as profitable as marketing Quisp or Wheaties or Wisk or Allstate or Maxwell House was thirty years ago. Sorry. Not my fault. But it's all we've got.

◉ **All of a sudden, it's obvious why you need a permission asset. If your company doesn't have one yet, you can start today, for free, by using Outlook on your PC. Give people an email address to write to. Write back. You're on your way.**

SETH GODIN

WHAT IT MEANS TO BE A MARKETER TODAY

If Purple Cow is now one of the *P*s of marketing, it has profound implications for the enterprise. It changes the definition of marketing.

It used to be that Engineering invented, Manufacturing built, Marketing marketed, and Sales sold. There was a clear division of labor, and the president managed the whole shebang. The marketer got a budget and she bought ads with it.

Marketing was really better called "advertising." Marketing was about communicating the values of a product after it had been developed and manufactured.

That's clearly not a valid strategy in a world where the product attributes (everything from service to design) are now at the heart of what it means to be a marketer. Marketing is the act of inventing the product. The effort of designing it. The craft of producing it. The art of pricing it. The technique of selling it. How can a Purple Cow company *not* be run by a marketer?

Companies that create Purple Cows—companies like JetBlue, Starbucks, Hasbro, and Poland Spring—have to be run by marketers. Turns out that the CEO of JetBlue made one critical decision on day one: He got the head of Marketing involved in product design and training as well. It shows. Everything they do that adds value is marketing. Poland Spring starts with worthless water. Hasbro starts with a few cents' worth of plastic and paper. JetBlue sells a commodity just like American Airlines does, but manages to make a profit doing it. These companies are marketers at their core.

The geniuses who invented 1-800-COLLECT are true marketers. They didn't figure out how to market an existing service. Instead, the marketing is built into the product—from the easy-to-remember phone number, of course, to the very idea that MCI could steal the collect call business from the pay-phone operators.

But isn't the same idea true for a local restaurant, a grinding wheel company, and Travelers Insurance? In a world where just about anything we need is good enough, and where just about all the profit comes from the Purple Cow, we're all marketers!

If a company is failing, it is the fault of the most senior management, and the problem is probably this: They're running a company, not marketing a product.

◉ **Go take a design course. Send your designers to a marketing course. And both of you should spend a week in the factory.**

Marketers No Longer:
Now We're Designers

Fifteen years ago, when Jerry Hirschberg was starting up the U.S. design studio for Nissan, he was invited to the long-range product planning meetings as an observer —a courtesy extended to him by the marketing people.

The meetings were all about vague pronouncements about future cars ("all entry-level cars should be as generic as possible") and plenty of spreadsheets about advertising spending and projected income. They were also the most important meetings the company held to plan its long-term future. The designers were mere tacticians.

Jerry proved, in short order, that he was much more than an observer. He demonstrated that designers not only had an important role in this process but should in fact dominate it.

If post-design, post-manufacture marketing is dead, what replaces it? Design. Not the pure design that they teach at Parsons, but a market-centric design that builds the very success of the product's marketing into the product itself.

The semantics get funky, but the facts are clear. The person with real influence on the success of a product today gets to sit at the table when the original seeds for a project are being sown.

If you are a marketer who doesn't know how to invent, design, influence, adapt, and ultimately discard products, then you're no longer a marketer. You're deadwood.

◉ **Make a list of all the remarkable products in your industry. Who made them? How did they happen? Model the behavior (not mimic the product) and you're more than halfway to making your own.**

WHAT DOES HOWARD KNOW?

One thing about Starbucks is obvious — the coffee is really and truly delicious. The reason is simple. Howard Schultz (the company's CEO) loves coffee. He refers to everyone who hasn't had their first cup of the day as "pre-caffeinated." He spent months in Italy, drinking and learning. He has a coffee *otaku*.

Where does remarkable come from? Often, it comes from passionate people who are making something for themselves. The Burton snowboard, the Vanguard mutual fund, the Apple iPod, and the Learjet all came from people with an *otaku*. It's interesting to note that the chocolate at Starbucks isn't as great as the coffee. Obviously, Howard doesn't know chocolate the way he knows coffee. Starbucks isn't obsessed with chocolate; they just serve it. Are you obsessed or just making a living?

The number-one question about the Purple Cow is, "How do I know it's remarkable?" This question almost always comes from the people who don't have the *otaku*. John Scharffenberger, founder of Scharffen Berger Chocolate, has no trouble telling great chocolate from ordinary chocolate. He gets it.

When I was building my first company (we created books), I always asked potential employees how often they went to the bookstore. People who don't love shopping for books obviously don't have the book *otaku*, and they're going to have a harder time inventing books for people who do.

Everyone who works at Patagonia is an outdoor nut. When the surf is up, the offices empty out as people rush to hit the waves. While this makes for a chaotic work environment, it also makes it more likely that Patagonia staff will know a remarkable outdoor product when they see one.

Compare this to the people who work at General Foods or General Mills or Kellogg's. A few of them might be obsessed with their products, but most of them just churn the stuff out. Imagine how cool Pop Tarts would be if the brand manager was the sort of person who ate them for dinner.

This is Dineh Mohajer, founder of Hard Candy, a cosmetics company with more than $10 million a year in sales. She knows what young women who love nail polish want because she is a young woman who loves nail polish.

A doctor I know makes a point of calling patients even if it's not bad news. If your routine tests come back with nothing to worry about, he calls and tells you. This is a monumentally simple task, but it's remarkable nonetheless. "It's simple," he told me; "that's what I want my doctor to do for me." Sometimes, in the middle of all the tumult of work, it's easy to forget that we're making something for people who care.

The challenge is in projecting. It's easier if you care deeply. But what if *you* don't care? What if you're busy making and marketing something you're not passionate about using? After all, someone needs to make disposable diapers or dialysis machines or grinding wheels.

You can choose from two techniques. The first is to learn the *art* of projecting. Of getting inside the heads of the people who *do* care deeply about this product and making them something they'll love and want to share. Marketers and designers who do it can put themselves into other people's shoes and imagine what *they'd* want. In the long run, learning this knack is actually much more profitable than being able to make stuff for only yourself. Learning this knack gives you more flexibility. There are marketers who can create Purple Cows for only a tiny audience—an audience just like the marketers themselves. They make decisions based on gut instinct, and (for a while) this works. If you follow this path, though, sooner or later your gut will let you down. If you haven't developed the humility that comes from being able to project to multiple audiences, you're likely to panic when you can't connect to your chosen group any longer.

The second technique is to learn the *science* of projecting—to build a discipline of launching products, watching, measuring, learning, and doing it again. Obviously, this technique doesn't work for complicated, long-sales-cycle products like jet airliners, but it does work for cars, toys, and most everything in between. Every February, the toy industry launches hundreds of toys at the annual Toy Fair. Only a fraction ever get produced, though. The non-remarkable ones disappear some time between their introduction and their ship date.

The marketers who are practicing the science of projecting what people want don't have a particular bias or point of view. Instead, they understand the *process* and will take it wherever it goes.

◉ **Is there someone (a person, an agency?) in your industry who has a track record of successfully launching remarkable products? Can you hire them away, or at least learn from their behavior? Immerse yourself in fan magazines, trade shows, design reviews—whatever it takes to feel what your fans feel.**

◉ **Can you create a culture of aggressively prototyping new products and policies? When GM shows a concept car at the New York Auto Show, there's more than ego involved. They're trying to figure out what car nuts think is remarkable. I'm not pitching focus groups here (they're a waste). I'm talking about very public releases of cheap prototypes.**

Do You Have to Be Outrageous to Be Remarkable?

Outrageous is not always remarkable. It's certainly not required. Sometimes outrageous is just annoying. Ozzy Osbourne is lucky to be both outrageous and remarkable. But a performance artist smearing himself with lard and wrapping himself in felt is just plain weird.

It's easy to fall into a trap of running upside-down ads, wearing green bow ties, and filling your ads with scatological references. Being scandalous might work on occasion, but it's not a strategy; it's desperation. The outrageousness needs to have a purpose, and it needs to be built into the product.

Walking onto a cross-country flight, I noticed that the 60-year-old woman in front of me was wearing a Hooters T-shirt. Their slogan? "Delightfully tacky, yet unrefined." The fascinating thing about Hooters' outrageousness is that it's just outrageous enough to be remarkable to this audience...without offending. Does everyone like Hooters? No way. That's part of what makes it remarkable. If everyone liked it, it would be boring.

The reminder: It's not about the way you say it, it's what you say. And while you can momentarily use offensive behavior to capture the attention of people who might not want to pay attention, it's not a long-run strategy. Outrageousness by itself won't work because the conversations sneezers have about you aren't positive.

◉ **You're probably guilty of being too shy, not too outrageous. Try being outrageous, just for the sake of being annoying. It's good practice. Don't do it too much because it doesn't usually work. But it's a good way to learn what it feels like to be at the edge.**

CASE STUDY: McDONALD'S FRANCE

The French subsidiary of McDonald's recently subsidized and publicized a report that urged the French not to visit fast-food outlets like McDonald's more than once a week. The report created a worldwide uproar, and the U.S. parent company professed to be "shocked!"

Is this a bad strategy? Perhaps by being honest (and very different) when talking to their customers, the French subsidiary is building the foundation of a long-term growth strategy. The American factory/advertising model demands more, more, more, which ultimately leads to a flameout when the pace of growth can't be maintained. By acknowledging the downsides of the fast-food experience, perhaps McDonald's France is reaching a far larger audience than they could ever hope to reach the old way.

◉ **What would happen if you told the truth?**

BUT WHAT ABOUT THE FACTORY?

This is certainly the biggest objection to Purple Cow thinking. Your company has been successful. You grew (probably on the strength of the TV-industrial complex). You invested in people, policies, distribution, a product line, and a factory. A system that every employee has bought into — it's who you are.

And now, apparently overnight, nothing is working the way it should. If you're Burger King, you switch ad agencies (again). If you're Motorola, you lay off ten thousand people. Small companies suffer, too, but more quietly.

Most big companies think that marketing is in crisis. They see that what they used to do doesn't work the way it used to. They want to protect their huge investment in infrastructure, and they believe that fixing their marketing is the answer.

Your boss and your coworkers are likely to resist when you share the thoughts in this book. They'll point out that it's marketing's job to market — that good marketing could fix the products you've got now. You don't have *time* for remarkable products anyway, they say. You need success right now.

Well, if you don't have time to do it right, what makes you think you'll have time to do it over?

I wrote this book to give you ammunition to make your case. Give everyone a copy. Not just the Marketing department. Everybody. Let them see that every single industry is feeling the same pain you are. Perhaps they'll realize that the problem isn't in your advertising — it's much bigger than that.

Before you spend another dollar on another brain-dead ad campaign, trade show, or sales conference, spend some time with your engineers and your customers. Challenge your people to start with a blank sheet of paper and figure out what they'd do if they could do just about anything. If they weren't afraid of failing, what's the most audacious thing they'd try?

The new CEO of Best Buy, Brad Anderson, is a brilliant strategist. He's got a sharp eye for the key moments in the evolution of his company. He said, "Instead of selling what *we* wanted to sell, we sold what people wanted us to sell, and then figured out how to make money doing it. Every time we talked to our customers, they wanted us to follow the path that turned out to be the hardest possible path we could follow. And every time, that path was the right path."

Best Buy could have done what just about every other regional electronics retailer facing a slowdown does: Buy some more newspaper ads. Play with the pricing. Lay some people off. Whine a bit and buckle down. Instead, Best Buy opted to follow a harder path, one that led to a remarkable experience for the consumer. At first, this looked like a longer, slower way to make their business grow, but in retrospect, it was a lot faster (and a lot cheaper) than running a bunch of boring ads and staying just where they were.

◉ **Remarkable isn't always about changing the biggest machine in your factory. It can be the way you answer the phone, launch a new brand, or price a revision to your software. Getting in the habit of doing the "unsafe" thing every time you have the opportunity is the best way to learn to project — you get practice at seeing what's working and what's not.**

The Problem with Cheap

Cheap is one of the only remarkable items that never seems to run out of appeal. For just about any repeatedly purchased item, all other things being equal, the cheap one will gain market share.

The problem with cheap is that once you start, your competitor will likely play the same game. In an incremental price war, how will one player beat the other and still win economically? IKEA can do it. Wal-Mart can do it. Can you?

Cheap is a lazy way out of the battle for the Purple Cow. Cheap is the last refuge of a product developer or marketer who is out of great ideas.

The exception to this rule is the quantum leap in pricing. When a marketer can radically redefine the way a product is produced or delivered, and leapfrog the pricing of others, that can create a remarkable game-changing event.

The Purple Cow is not the exclusive domain of high-priced products and wealthy consumers. Motel 6 is remarkable for being simultaneously clean and cheap. Same with Wal-Mart.

JetBlue and Southwest have completely changed the pricing equation in air travel. Traditional carriers, with expensive hubs and awkward union relationships, cannot sustain long-term price competition. In the long run, the 50-percent cost advantage enjoyed by these new competitors is certain to defeat the old guard. American and United know this, yet there's absolutely nothing that they can do about it. Southwest changed the rules of the game, and the big airlines don't even have a pair of dice.

IKEA has done it in furniture. They so dominate their

segment with cheap (but not cheapo) furnishings that they are able to drive their costs lower and lower. Their volume advantage changes the game for their competition, guaranteeing IKEA leadership in this segment (until some competitor figures out a remarkable way to change the game again).

◉ **If you could build a competitor that had costs that were 30 percent lower than yours, could you do it? If you could, why don't you?**

CASE STUDY: WHAT SHOULD
HALLMARK.COM DO?

Hallmark runs one of the three biggest online greeting card services. The site grew when an ideavirus started — people would send an e-card to a friend, who would find out about the service by reading the card and would respond by sending a few more cards. Within a year, billions of cards were flying around online.

The challenge, of course, is turning this free activity into something that can actually make money. One thing that's working for Hallmark is selling gift certificates. Hallmark owns a gift certificate company, and they make a profit every time you spend $20 on a $20 gift certificate (complicated, but true).

Anyway, Hallmark lies at the nexus of three powerful forces at work in this book, so I was happy to help my friend at Hallmark brainstorm some ways to put them to work.

To start, Hallmark has permission to talk to the audience. These are consumers who voluntarily come to the site to send a card. No interruption media necessary. Alas, even though they are here on their own, many of them aren't looking for Hallmark to have a voice in the conversation, so they're not listening to any news Hallmark might want to share.

Fortunately, many of the visitors are members of Hallmark's Gold Crown Club. These consumers are busy collecting points (à la frequent flyer miles) to trade in for prizes. These self-selected consumers have a problem (how do I get more points?) that they're willing to look to the market to solve.

And best of all, these Gold Crown Club members are assiduous sneezers. They send a ton of cards (electronic and paper) every year, and the people they send them to enjoy receiving them — the recipients know the sender doesn't have anything to gain. They just care enough to send the very best.

The win, it seems to me, is for Hallmark to discover whether people getting a gift certificate are likely to turn around and send one. If the idea of an electronic gift certificate is remarkable enough to spread, then their challenge is to get the core group of sneezers to spread the word.

So here are my ideas for my friend at Hallmark:

When a Gold Crown Club member is about to send an e-card, ask him if he wants to find out how many points he'll get if he also sends a gift certificate. This will be a randomly chosen number between 100 points (a little) and 1 million points (a ton!). Obviously, most people will win a small number, but every once in a while someone will be eligible to win a large number.

Most members of this concentrated, focused, listening group will be happy to risk a click to get to the next page just to see how much they stand to earn. Now that Hallmark has shifted the conversation from "send an e-card" to "talk to Hallmark about gift certificates," Hallmark has a chance to sell these consumers on why a gift certificate might be a remarkable gift. And many of these sneezers—suitably motivated, rewarded, and educated—will go ahead and send one.

Of course, this promotion doesn't hit a home run unless recipients of the gift certificates start sending gift certificates as well.

Isn't a million points a lot to give away? Exactly. It's Purple.

When the Cow Looks for a Job

So far, we've talked about what companies should do. But what about you? Can you apply this thinking to your job search?

Odds are that the last time you switched jobs, you used a résumé. Following conventional wisdom, you may have sent it to hundreds or thousands of employers. You may have posted it online or emailed it in an effort to "network" your way to a new job.

All of this effort is really nothing but advertising. Advertising in a way that's very different from buying TV ads, but also very similar. After all, your résumé is likely to land on the desk of someone with no interest whatsoever in you or what you're up to. Worse, it's unlikely that this strategy will lead to much word of mouth.

There's another way. You've probably guessed it: Be exceptional. Remarkable people with remarkable careers seem to switch jobs with far less effort. Remarkable people often don't even have a résumé. Instead, they rely on sneezers who are quick to recommend them when openings come up. Remarkable people are often recruited from jobs they love to jobs they love even more.

The secret doesn't lie in the job-seeking technique. It has to do with what these people do when they're *not* looking for a job. These Purple Cows do an outrageous job. They work on high-profile projects. These people take risks, often resulting in big failures. These failures rarely lead to a dead end, though. They're not really risks, after all. Instead, they just increase the chances that these people will get an even better project next time.

If you're thinking about being a Purple Cow, the time to do it is when you're not looking for a job.

In your career, even more than for a brand, being safe is risky. The path to lifetime job security is to be remarkable.

◉ **References available upon request? Nonsense. Your references are your résumé. A standard résumé is nothing but an opportunity for a prospective employer to turn you down. A sheaf of over-the-top references, on the other hand, begs for a meeting.**

◉ **Visit www.monster.com. Millions of résumés, all in a pile, all waiting for someone to find them. If you're in that pile, it's not a good place to be. Before you start looking for a job, consider what you could do today so you never have to worry about that.**

Case Study: Tracey the Publicist

So my friend Tracey quit her job at a publicity firm to set up her own shop. Following conventional wisdom, she sent out hundreds of form letters to hundreds of marketing directors all over the Northeast. This is awfully expensive advertising, and of course, it didn't work very well.

Any marketing directors who *need* a PR firm probably already have one. If they were looking for a new one, it would take far more than an unsolicited FedEx package to get them to pick up the phone and call Tracey.

What to do?

After talking with Tracey, I suggested that she focus on the narrowest possible niche. Her background was in pharmaceuticals, so we picked that. In fact, we went way further—to plastic surgeons. Tracey decided to focus obsessively on being the world's best publicist to plastic surgeons. If pharmaceutical companies need to reach this audience in the most effective way, they'll need to call her. She knows all the journals, all the conferences, and most of the doctors. She has the lists and the contacts. She is the one and only exceptional choice. Everyone else has this audience as part of their portfolio. For Tracey, they *are* her portfolio.

If your job depended on hiring the best person in the world to publicize your new product to plastic surgeons, who would you hire?

CASE STUDY: ROBYN WATERS GETS IT

How long has it been since you've been to Kmart? My guess, if you're like most readers of this book, is "a long time." The same can't be said of Target, though. Target is the discounter of choice among professionals, design freaks, and serious shoppers (in other words, people with money to spend).

How did Target do it? It certainly wasn't their advertising — though that's pretty good. Nope, it's because of people like Robyn Waters, their VP of "trend, design, and technical specifications." (Yes, that's her actual title.)

Robyn is the person who persuaded Michael Graves to make a teapot for Target. She's the one who searches out amazingly cheap (but cool) flatware, and little pens with floating targets in them. Instead of spending time and money trying to buy market share with advertising, Target has realized that by offering exclusive items that would be cool at any price — but that are amazing when they're cheap — they can win *without* a big ad budget. Cool products that appeal to people who both buy new stuff and talk about it a lot are the core of Target's strategy.

If a big-box retailer like Target can obliterate Sears and Kmart, what's stopping you from being many degrees cooler than your bigger competitors?

Case Study: So Popular,
No One Goes There Anymore

Here's a great case study of how the Purple Cow cycle works.

Stew Leonard started an ordinary dairy store in Connecticut. It was less than twenty thousand square feet, selling milk, cheese, and the usual dairy store essentials. Stew didn't want to settle for a tiny store, though, so he embraced the Cow.

He put a petting zoo out front. He developed a customer service policy so simple and important he had it carved in a 6,000-pound block of granite and put in front of the store. He started featuring unique or unusual products, and he sold many items for dramatically reduced prices. The store was stuffed with robotic mooing cows, dancing milk cartons, and a violin-playing chicken.

As the suburbs near his Connecticut store grew, so did the legend of his Purple Cow. Stew expanded the store more than ten times, eventually showing up in *Ripley's Believe It or Not!* He was lauded in one of Tom Peters' major books. He was an advisor to politicians and a friend of Paul Newman. Stew also sold more Perdue chicken every day than did any other store in the world.

The store and the innovation it stood for were so spectacular that I took each and every employee I hired and drove them an hour north to Connecticut just to see how customer service and showmanship could combine to create a world-class organization.

That was ten years ago.

Today, Stew Leonard's is run by his son, and the store has expanded to several locations. One of them is just two miles from my house. I never go there.

Why?

Because it's too popular. And it's boring.

The new Stew (Stew Jr.) used the Purple Cow to spread the word and to grow. And it worked. But now that he has *already* spread the word, it's more profitable to milk the Cow. Stew exchanged me (someone with a food and service *otaku* and a big-time sneezer) for ten ordinary grocery consumers. The products at Stew's are no longer unique. He carries nothing organic, no brands you've never seen before, nothing at a remarkably low price. The customer service is merely okay. Ask someone in the fish department where to find canned pumpkin, and he'll point in a vague direction and say, "Over there." In the old days (when Stew's was still remarkable), someone would walk you over.

There used to be a suggestion box at the exit. If you submitted a suggestion, more often than not you got a letter back from Stew (Senior) himself. Today, the suggestion box is still there, but don't count on getting a letter back. The business is too profitable to worry about that.

So . . . when your parking lot is full to bursting, and you're making far more money than you ever did before, does that mean you don't have to worry about the Cow?

In the short run, Stew Junior's strategy is brilliant. He's using the brand his father built and creating significant wealth. It's cynical but it's true—dumbing down his store for the masses (not the sneezers) was the way to get rich in a hurry. If your business is in a similar situation, your shareholders probably want you to do precisely the same thing.

The grocery business is pretty special in that once you stake out a location, you can profit from it for a very long time. There's also not much chance that grocery stores are going to go out of style, so your ride on top is pretty long indeed.

If, on the other hand, your goals are growth and impact and building an ever-larger and sustained business, it's hard to imagine how this strategy scales. If Stew opens a store in Houston, Texas (an area well-served by big supermarkets and where virtually no one has heard of Stew's Purple Cow), he's just not going to do very well. And if Stew's business was as subject to the vagaries of fashion as yours is, he'd have more to worry about as well.

The Purple Cow is just part of the product life cycle. You can't live it all the time (too risky, too expensive, too tiring), but when you need to grow or need to introduce something new, it's your best shot.

Next time you go to Stew's, say hi for me. You'll find me and my friends at Brother's, the fast-growing, very profitable, and quite remarkable vegetable market around the corner.

IS IT ABOUT PASSION?

My hero Tom Peters asks, "Does the work matter?" The idea of adding passion and Wow! and magic to what we do is compelling to many of us. All of the great ideation and risk-taking and multidisciplinary magic that Tom and those who followed him have riffed about are so important — but they don't appeal to many of the people we work with.

The people who say, "How can we make it appeal to a broader audience?" or "Wal-Mart won't take it," or "We can't afford silly meetings or product failures" aren't being moved by the heroic tales of innovative marketers. The skeptics think the whole passion thing is sort of flaky. They're not buying it. Nope, those people don't care about the *why*. They just want to do what's going to work.

And that's the point of the Cow. You don't have to like it. You don't have to be a *Fast Company* junkie, a new-product guru, a make-work-matter apostle. No, you just have to realize that *nothing else is working*. The proof is there. The big brands, the big successes, the profitable start-ups (big and small, worldwide and local) have all (okay mostly) been about the Cow.

You don't need passion to create a Purple Cow. Nor do you need an awful lot of creativity. What you need is the insight to realize that you have no other choice but to grow your business or launch your product with Purple Cow thinking. *Nothing else is going to work.*

That means that launching ten products for $10 million each is a lot smarter than investing $100 million in TV to launch just one product. It means that if all ten products fail, you've just learned ten ways that aren't going to work. You're still ahead of where you'd be if the one TV launch had failed (which is far more likely than not.)

If your boss wants focus groups to prove that a new product is guaranteed to be a success, don't bother. If the focus group likes it, they're probably wrong. If your company wants you to pick one and only one product to feature this Christmas, start working on your résumé. You're not going to invent a Purple Cow with those sorts of odds and that kind of pressure. Things that *have* to work rarely do anymore.

You don't need a book about creativity or brainstorming or team building. You've already got a hundred (or a thousand) ideas your group doesn't have the guts to launch. You don't need more time or even more money. You just need the realization that a brand new business paradigm is now in charge, and once you accept the reality of the Cow, finding one suddenly gets much easier.

J. Peterman knew how to reach *New Yorker* readers. He knew it was too late to become Lillian Vernon, so he didn't try. For the audience he was targeting, his catalog and his voice were magical. No big mail-order company would have invested in his vision at first. Too untested, too "unusual." Some might even call it weird.

When Comedy Central focus-group-tested *South Park*, it set a record, scoring just 1.5 out of 10 points with women. Three of the women in the group cried, they hated it so much. Scary? Sure. Weird? To some. But the group that mattered—adolescent boys and those who act like them—spread the word, and the show was a monster hit.

Remember, it's not about being weird. It's about being irresistible to a tiny group of easily reached sneezers with *otaku*. Irresistible isn't the same as ridiculous. Irresistible (for the right niche) is just remarkable.

TRUE FACTS

Interbrand values the top one hundred brands in the world every year. Interbrand combines a bunch of mysterious factors and determines which brands are worth the most. Here's the list for 2002:

1. Coca-Cola	35. Nike	69. Rolex
2. Microsoft	36. Gap	70. Time
3. IBM	37. Heinz	71. Ericsson
4. GE	38. Volkswagen	72. Tiffany
5. Intel	39. Goldman Sachs	73. Levi's
6. Nokia	40. Kellogg's	74. Motorola
7. Disney	41. Louis Vuitton	75. Duracell
8. McDonald's	42. SAP	76. BP
9. Marlboro	43. Canon	77. Hertz
10. Mercedes	44. IKEA	78. Bacardi
11. Ford	45. Pepsi	79. Caterpillar
12. Toyota	46. Harley	80. Amazon.com
13. Citibank	47. MTV	81. Panasonic
14. HP	48. Pizza Hut	82. Boeing
15. Amex	49. KFC	83. Shell
16. Cisco Systems	50. Apple	84. Smirnoff
17. AT&T	51. Xerox	85. Johnson & Johnson
18. Honda	52. Gucci	86. Prada
19. Gillette	53. Accenture	87. Moët & Chandon
20. BMW	54. L'Oreal	88. Heineken
21. Sony	55. Kleenex	89. Mobil
22. Nescafé	56. Sun	90. Burger King
23. Oracle	57. Wrigley's	91. Nivea
24. Budweiser	58. Reuters	92. *Wall Street Journal*
25. Merrill Lynch	59. Colgate	93. Starbucks
26. Morgan Stanley	60. Philips	94. Barbie
27. Compaq	61. Nestlé	95. Ralph Lauren
28. Pfizer	62. Avon	96. FedEx
29. JPMorgan	63. AOL	97. Johnnie Walker
30. Kodak	64. Chanel	98. Jack Daniel's
31. Dell	65. Kraft	99. 3M
32. Nintendo	66. Danone	100. Armani
33. Merck	67. Yahoo!	
34. Samsung	68. adidas	

Of these top one hundred, seventy are brands that were valuable in this country more than twenty-five years ago. Of these brands, virtually all were built with heavy advertising on television, in magazines, or at retail. These companies grew their brands back when it was easy and cheap to do it the old-fashioned way. These brands maintain their lead, blocking newcomers who don't have the same vacuum to fill.

Of the remaining thirty brands, half were built almost entirely through word of mouth (Hewlett-Packard, Oracle, Nintendo, SAP, Canon, IKEA, Sun, Yahoo!, Ericsson, Motorola, Amazon.com, Prada, Starbucks, Polo Ralph Lauren, and Armani). While some of these brands—like Lauren and Sun—spent heavily on print advertising, it's pretty clear that without a remarkable product and significant word of mouth, they wouldn't have acquired the value and cachet they now hold.

That leaves just fifteen brands. Some, like Cisco Systems and Microsoft, acquired their value through market power (either by acquiring competitors or bullying them out of the way). Others, like Apple, used both remarkable advertising *and* word of mouth. That leaves only a tiny handful (Compaq, Dell, Nike, The Gap, MTV, AOL, and perhaps Nivea) that built their brands the old-fashioned way. I'd argue that MTV doesn't really count since they advertised only on their own channel, which people found through word of mouth.

Notice that just one of the companies on the list is the product of the last ten years of media excess. Only AOL was able to spend hundreds of millions of dollars and convert that investment into a valuable brand. All the other companies that tried, failed.

So the question you need to ask yourself is this: If only 6 percent of the most valuable brands used the now-obsolete strategy of constantly reminding us about their sort-of-ordinary product, why do you believe this strategy will work for you?

◉ **The big question is this: Do you want to grow? If you do, you need to embrace the Cow. You can maintain your brand the old way, but the only route to healthy growth is a remarkable product.**

BRAINSTORMS

While we can't predict what's going to be remarkable next time, we can realize that there aren't too many unexplored areas of innovation — just unexplored combinations. Here's an annotated checklist. With just thirty-four examples, it's not complete by any means, but it might get your juices flowing.

While this checklist may elicit an "of course," I wonder how many struggling products have actually been through this analysis. Is your most recent offering the *mostest* of any of these attributes?

———

WHEN I WENT TO BUY SOME NEW TOOLS, I did something I almost never do. I went to Sears. Why? Because almost without exception, the people I like and trust who spend a lot of time with tools told me that I couldn't go wrong with Craftsman. Why? Not because they're beautifully designed or easy to use. Solely because they last a long time and are guaranteed forever. KitchenAid, on the other hand, has lost legions of sneezing bakers because the company decided to save money in the way they make their mixers. Online bulletin boards are filled with stories of frustrated people who quit the brand after going through three or four mixers. In both cases, the stories are based on remarkable durability (or the lack thereof).

———

THE OXO LINE of kitchen gadgets sells to people who don't even cook. Why? Because these non-cooks have visited the kitchens of people who do cook. And those cooking sneezers (always open to something that would make their lives in the kitchen better) were delighted to show off their funky-looking (and very, very functional) carrot peelers, lime zesters, and ice cream scoopers.

WHY DID YAHOO! defeat AltaVista, Lycos, and Infoseek in the race to become the center of the Internet? And how did Yahoo! forget that lesson and let Google do it again? In each case, Yahoo! and Google had the same things going for them. Unbelievably simple interface (for the first few years of Google, there were only two buttons—and one of them was "I feel lucky"). Fast loading. No decisions. When people asked someone else where to go to get what they needed online, the recommendation was simple.

Here's a great Google story I heard from Mark Hurst: It turns out that the folks at Google are obsessed with the email they get criticizing the service. They take it very seriously. One person writes in every once in a while, and he never signs his name. According to Marissa Meyer at Google, "Every time he writes, the e-mail contains only a two-digit number. It took us awhile to figure out what he was doing. Turns out he's counting the number of words on the home page. When the number goes up, like up to 52, it gets him irritated, and he e-mails us the new word count. As crazy as it sounds, his e-mails are helpful, because it has put an interesting discipline on the UI team, so as not to introduce too many links. It's like a scale that tells you that you've gained two pounds." (Yahoo! has more than five hundred words on their home page now.)

———

A LONG TIME AGO, Hertz and Avis grew their brands with TV and print advertising. Today, it's too late for their competitors to catch up using the same technique. So National and Alamo struggle. Enterprise Rental Car, though, has an entirely different strategy. They're not at the airport and they don't cater to business travelers. Instead, they created a new Purple Cow—they'll pick you up with a rental car when your regular car is in the shop or totaled in an accident.

Targeting this niche seems obvious, but the ability to be radically different has also made them profitable and fast-growing. Safe, it seems, is risky.

———•———

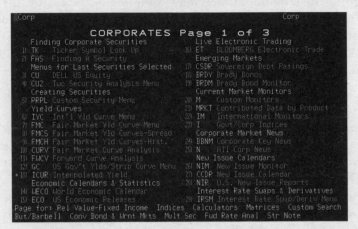

THE BLOOMBERG, AS IT'S KNOWN, should have been replaced by the Internet, yet this customized computer is on the desk of just about every important player on Wall Street. After all, the Net has access to huge amounts of information, it's relatively easy to use, there are multiple sources for it, and it's largely free. The Bloomberg, on the other hand, is very expensive (more than a $1,000 a month) and very tricky to use. And that's why traders and other investors insist on it. They've gone through the pain of learning how to use it, and they're not prepared to give up that expertise.

———•———

WHY DOES TED LEONSIS, billionaire owner of the Washington Wizards, stay at the Four Seasons in Manhattan? I mean, he could stay anywhere he wants to. As best as I can tell, he stays there because the entire staff at the café knows how to bring him his iced tea. In a tall thin glass, with ice, with a little carafe of hyper-sweet sugar water on the side. He doesn't ask for it; they just bring it. Every person who meets with Ted at the hotel notices it. I think it makes Ted happy that his friends notice it. Having something personalized can make one feel special.

—·—

L.L. BEAN CAN SELL mail-order clothes to people who don't trust mail order. It's the guarantee that makes it work. Take a pair of pants, light them on fire, send in the ashes, and L.L. Bean will refund your money. Stories like that make it easy for a sneezer to spread the word.

—·—

WHAT KIND OF MOTORCYCLE does Shaquille O'Neal own? Jesse Gregory James is a maker of custom motorcycles — giant, $100,000 bikes. Each motorcycle is handmade, months in the making, and very, very profitable. And there's a multi-year waiting list. Someone who can afford a motorcycle that costs this much wants (and probably deserves) to have it made just for him. The act of making something very expensive and very custom is in itself remarkable.

—·—

THE HUMMER IS TOO BIG, too wide, too ugly, and too inefficient to be a car. It doesn't belong on public roads. It annoys most of the people who come in contact with it. Except, of course, for the people who buy it. Most of them don't need to suddenly go off-road and climb steep, sandy hills. Hummer drivers just like annoying the rest of us. They enjoy driving a truly remarkable vehicle.

—·—

WHY DO MOVIE EXECUTIVES fly halfway across the world to the Cannes Film Festival? While the parties are fun, they can't possibly make up for the inconvenience and investment of time and money. The reason is simple —the executives know that something remarkable will happen there. Some movie, some director, some star will make news. The movie executives will discover something new, and that's why they go. How can your product make news? (Note that there's a big difference between making the news and making news. Forcing your way onto TV with publicity hype is not much of a long-term strategy. It works a lot better when you've actually got something to say.)

———

WHERE DID MY SON GO to get his new pet? Well, type in "frog pet" on Google and you'll find growafrog.com, the Web site for a twenty-year-old company that does just one thing: it sells pet tadpoles (soon to be frogs) in little plastic aquariums. My son has already told twenty other friends about these guys, and the little booklet of frog lore they include makes it even easier to share. (Did you know that some of the frogs they sell live to be seventeen years old?) This company's obsessive focus on this niche made them the obvious choice.

Just like the two stores in New York: one is called Just Bulbs; the other is called Just Shades. No, they're not related. No, they're not near each other. But yes, they're pretty remarkable.

———

YES, YOU'VE HEARD IT ABOUT VOLVO BEFORE, but the fact remains that a tiny country created a car with a profitable niche because the country made it so easy for sneezers to sell to those who didn't realize what they were missing. The fact that the Volvo was widely considered to be ugly was the perfect conversation starter. The fact that you've heard this story a hundred times before proves that it works.

———

DO YOU REMEMBER THE LONG BOX? A ten-inch-long
sleeve of cardboard, it encased CDs for years. Record companies thought the extra cardboard would give them more
marketing space, while retailers figured they would cut down
on theft. Some artists, though, complained. In addition to
consumers' hating the packaging, the artists pointed out that
millions of trees were being needlessly killed to print this
disposable packaging, and landfills were filling up with the
debris. One of the reasons this campaign succeeded was that
it wasn't a very big concession for anyone along the way. It
was easy news to spread, and easier still for big companies to
appear to be environmentally sensitive by giving in to the
threats of boycott and ceasing production of the long box.

WHILE COMPUTERS ARE the obvious example of how
technology can make a product remarkable, how about
handmade watches? Some watch manufacturers charge
upwards of $50,000 for devices that can be wound just
once a week, track the phases of the moon, and automati-
cally remember leap year fifty years in the future. Amazingly, the more complex the watch, the longer the waiting
list. The most complicated watch built today has a waiting
list of more than two years. No, it's not a mass-market
item, but it sells because it's complicated (if the buyer
wanted accuracy and features, he'd buy a $50 Casio).

COMEDIAN BUDDY HACKETT learned a long time ago
that when he didn't have anything funny to say, he should
just swear. People liked that. Today, we see movies and
records and books and bars that succeed just because they
intentionally cross the boundaries of good taste. The best
example is John Waters. His first movies were so gross,
most people consider them unwatchable. Not the early
adopters with a taste for the bizarre. They rushed to tell

their friends, and Waters' reputation was made. Today, *Hairspray*, based on his movie of the same name, is the hottest play on Broadway. Many of those who tread a more culturally acceptable path to get to the same end have not succeeded nearly as well.

———

A RESTAURANT NEAR MY HOUSE hired a teenager to wear a clown suit and do magic tricks and create balloon animals all weekend, every weekend. The result is pretty predictable. Kids told kids, parents told parents, and the restaurant was packed with families every weekend. It wasn't hard, but it was remarkable.

———

WHEN BEST BUY CHANGED their product (the store!) and got rid of the commissions, that set the stage for a growth spurt that took them from $250 million in annual revenue to more than $23 billion. A retailer does more than just move boxes. A retailer sells, with the environment and the people who work there. Best Buy made their sales technique so different it was noteworthy.

———

OTHER THAN ITS MUCH FABLED open-source origins, why does Linux have such a following? One reason is that becoming a Linux user requires a real commitment. Linux is hard to install, hard to use without a lot of practice, and not easy to integrate into a traditional corporate environment. All of these hurdles, though, created a devoted and loyal core. This group realized that as they got more and more people to invest their time in using and supporting the product, the operating system would get better, investments would be made in software and user interfaces, and internal issues would disappear. The flaws in the product itself created an asset.

———

MOST TOWNS HAVE ONE: a steakhouse that serves a three-pound steak for $50-and then refunds your money if you can finish it. Word gets out. People come. Not to eat the steak (that would be stupid) but because the message behind it is fairly remarkable. The same thing happens with ski resorts with very difficult slopes and with video services that let you rent as many DVDs as you want.

THERE'S MORE RISK than ever in our lives. That's one reason so many businesses ship Federal Express. When L.L. Bean switched, it wasn't so much because people wanted their orders delivered faster. It was because the certainty of the delivery date and the ability to track the package in real time gave people needed assurance.

DO YOU REALLY THINK that any one of the ten people who will buy out the entire production run of the world's fastest motorcycle (0 to 250 miles an hour in 14 seconds) will ever take it to top speed? Of course not. But for $250,000, they sure could. Is your product the best at anything worth measuring?

WHAT HAPPENS WHEN part of your product or service breaks? How soon before someone shows up to fix it? When my PowerBook broke, I called Apple. Two hours later, an Airborne Express truck pulled up with a cardboard shipping box and took my Mac away —and they brought it back 48 hours later! Wow.

This isn't a stunt, nor is it foolish altruism. Apple profits by selling AppleCare (insurance that they'll be there if your machine breaks) and they enjoy the word of mouth that a story like this generates.

THERE IS ACTUALLY A CONTEST for the loudest car stereo. These stereos are so loud that you can't get into the car — you'd go deaf. The current champ is eight times louder than a 747 jet. Yet people spend hundreds of thousands of dollars in their quest for the loudest stereo. And thousands of other people buy the winning brands — not to play them quite that loud, but just to know they could.

———

AT THE OTHER END OF THE SPECTRUM, people pay extraordinary premiums for the last decibel of noise reduction if they believe it matters to them. Quiet windows, buildings, neighborhoods, laptops, cars — in each case, the amount spent for each incremental decibel of noise reduction is often double what the previous one cost. Watch one traveler busy selling a seatmate on the Bose noise-limiting headphones, and you can see the ideavirus at work.

———

IKEA IS NOT JUST ANOTHER cheap furniture store. There are plenty of places to buy stuff that's cheap. But most of them can't offer the brilliant combination of form and function you get for the same price at IKEA. Last year, the chain sold more than 25 percent of all the furniture sold in its price range in Europe and the United States. That stunning figure isn't the result of advertising. It's clearly a response to IKEA's market-beating combination of quality and price.

———

LOTTERY TICKETS OFFER low investment and a big win. When the jackpot hits record levels ($100 million is remarkable money, even to a millionaire), ticket sales go up exponentially. Ironically, the odds of winning are even worse than usual, so buying when there's a $20 million jackpot is the smarter of two dumb choices. So why do sales go up? Because the remarkable nature of the larger jackpot gets people talking about it and dreaming about winning.

———

WHY DO SOME PEOPLE smoke unfiltered cigarettes or drink high-proof alcohol? Maybe it's the affiliation with danger and self-destruction. The extreme nature of the product makes it appealing to this audience.

———

WHEN A PRODUCT OR SERVICE is about risk avoidance, a solution that minimizes that risk is worth talking about. If I were a lawyer, I'd specialize in a very narrow niche, becoming the best in the world at defending a certain kind of lawsuit. If your company was the victim of one of these lawsuits, whom would you hire? The specialist who does nothing but defend (and win) cases like this, or your local corporate firm? When someone has a problem like this, he is extremely open to external marketing messages, and he will seek out and usually find someone who presents him with the lowest possible downside.

———

WHY GO KITEBOARDING? I mean, you can ski or snow-board or windsurf or water-ski. Yet kiteboarding is one of the fastest-growing sports today. Strap a surfboard to your feet, hold onto a huge kite, and start racing across the water at thirty miles an hour. Unless, of course, you get dragged along the beach. So dangerous, it's worth talking about. So dangerous that those who seek out new and dangerous sports are drawn to it.

———

IF YOU'VE EVER BEEN TO SOTHEBY'S or a Soho art gallery, you'll notice that almost without exception, the men and women working there are truly beautiful. Not just beautiful on the inside, but really good looking. I wonder why that is. What would happen if your nuts-and-bolts plumbing supply company hired a beautiful male model as a receptionist? People would talk.

———

SPEEDING THROUGH THE AIRPORT the other day, I noticed that the clothing worn by just about everyone working at every concession was totally unremarkable. Why not dress the folks at the ice cream stand in pink and white stripes and bow ties? "Hey, did you see that?"

———

EASILY OVERLOOKED, but just as important as physical appearance, is the voice that people hear. I respond differently when I hear James Earl Jones welcoming me to Directory Assistance. Moviefone succeeded in its early days largely as a result of curious people calling to hear what their friends called "that annoying voice."

———

I LOVE MY DOCTOR. Not just because I'm not sick (which is partly his doing) but also because he spends so much time with me when I visit. I don't think Ray does this as a marketing tool — I think he really and truly cares. And it's remarkable. Remarkable enough that I've referred a dozen patients to him.

———

NO ONE WILL ARGUE YOU WITH YOU if you claim that Wal-Mart is the biggest, most profitable, scariest retailer on earth. So, when Wal-Mart was frantically trying to catch up with Amazon.com, what did they have plastered on a banner in their offices? "You can't out-Amazon Amazon."

It's a great insight. Even this mighty retailer realized that just copying Amazon's strengths wouldn't be sufficient. Once someone stakes out a limit, you're foolish to attempt a pail imitation. The Democrats will never be able to out-Republican the Republicans, Reebok can't out-Nike Nike and JetBlue didn't try to out-American American. You have to go where the competition is not. The farther the better.

———

DOES THE POSTAL SERVICE hire annoying people or just train them to be that way? How many times have you told someone about a bad experience at the Motor Vehicles bureau? It's not expensive, and if you're not really and truly a monopoly, it might be worth investing in exceptionally nice people as a way of being remarkable.

———

EVERYONE KNOWS that the record business is dying, that no smart entrepreneur would start a real business trying to make money in music. Don't tell that to Micah Solomon, David Glasser or Derek Sivers. Micah runs Oasis CD Duplication, which is obsessed with making CDs for independent musicians. One example of his remarkable behavior: He regularly sends a sampler CD to every important radio station in the country—and the CD only includes music from his customers.

David Glasser and his partners run Airshow Mastering, which creates cutting edge CD masters for Sony—and for individual musicians as well. He does an amazing job in helping musicians realize their dreams.

And where do both companies send these musicians when the records are ready to be sold? To CDBaby.com, the best record store on the web. Derek sells the work of literally thousands of independent acts, doing it with such success (and treating his partners with such respect) that word of mouth is the only advertising he needs to attract new musicians and new customers.

A quick visit to CDBaby.com, oasiscd.com and airshow-mastering.com will make it clear just how remarkable these three companies are. They understand that they have a choice between distinct or extinct.

Will any business that targets a dying business succeed? Of course not. But these three prove that targeting a thriving niche in a slow-moving industry can work—if you're prepared to invest what it takes to be remarkable.

AT BROCK'S RESTAURANT in Stamford, Connecticut, here's what it says on the menu (in large type):

SORRY-NO SHARING SALAD BAR

IN ORDER TO KEEP OUR OVERALL PRICING REASONABLE, IT IS IMPORTANT THAT AN HONOR SYSTEM OF NO SHARING OF THE SALAD BAR BE RESPECTED. SHOULD YOU CHANGE YOUR MIND AND WISH TO ENJOY THE SALAD BAR, IT IS ONLY 2.95 WITH A SANDWICH, BURGER OR ENTREE. FOR YOUR UNDERSTANDING AND COOPERATION WE THANK YOU.

Compare this to the wine policy at a restaurant called Frontière. The owner puts an open bottle of wine on every table, and at the end of the meal you tell the waiter how many glasses you consumed. The honor system.

Which is more worthy of positive comment? Marketing benefits aside, which leads to more incremental profit? (Hint: Two glasses of wine pay for a whole bottle at wholesale!)

GODIN'S THIRD LAW of restaurant dining points out that the friendliness of the staff at a pizza place is inversely proportional to the quality. At Johnny's Pizza in Mt.

Vernon, NY, they were still yelling at me after five years of being a regular. At Louis's hamburger shack in New Haven, they will absolutely refuse to serve you ketchup with your hamburger—a fact well-chronicled on Web sites and by word of mouth. And of course, Al Yeganeh, a wonderful, misunderstood soup entrepreneur, has people waiting in line for hours to buy his Lobster Bisque. Misread the rules, and no soup for you. Could you improve the fame of your retail establishment by creating stupid rules and hiring truly mean waiters? Sure, probably.

◎ **Explore the limits. What if you're the cheapest, the fastest, the slowest, the hottest, the coldest, the easiest, the most efficient, the loudest, the most hated, the copycat, the outsider, the hardest, the oldest, the newest, the . . . most! If there's a limit, you should (must) test it.**

Salt is Not Boring–Eight More Ways to Bring the Cow to Work

For fifty years, Morton has made salt a boring commodity. People at their headquarters would happily agree with you that there was no possibility of a Purple Cow in this business.

Good thing the folks who create handmade salt from seawater in France didn't know that. They regularly get $20 a pound for their amazing salt. The Hawaiians have just entered the market as well, creating a stir at gourmet restaurants. Now, ordinarily boring Diamond Kosher salt is looking at millions of dollars in increased annual sales–because their salt tastes better on food.

◉ **Is your product more boring than salt? Unlikely. So come up with a list of ten ways to change the product (not the hype) to make it appeal to a sliver of your audience.**

◉ **Think small. One vestige of the TV-industrial complex is a need to think mass. If it doesn't appeal to everyone, the thinking goes, it's not worth it. No longer. Think of the smallest conceivable market, and describe a product that overwhelms it with its remarkability. Go from there.**

◉ **Outsource. If the factory is giving you a hard time about jazzing up the product, go elsewhere. There are plenty of job shops that would be delighted to take on your product. After it works, the factory will probably be happy to take the product back.**

◉ **Build and use a permission asset. Once you have the ability to talk directly to your most loyal customers, it gets much easier to develop and sell** amazing things. Without the filters of advertising, wholesalers, and retailers, you can create products that are far more remarkable.

◎ Copy. Not from your industry, but from any other industry. Find an industry more dull than yours, discover who's remarkable (it won't take long), and do what they did.

◎ Go one more. Or two more. Identify a competitor who's generally regarded as at the edges, and outdo them. Whatever they're known for, do that thing even more. Even better, and even safer, do the opposite of what they're doing.

◎ Find things that are "just not done" in your industry, and do them. JetBlue almost instituted a dress code for passengers. They're still playing with the idea of giving a free airline ticket to the best-dressed person on the plane. A plastic surgeon could offer gift certificates. A book publisher could put a book on sale. Stew Leonard's took the strawberries out of the little green plastic cages and let the customers pick their own — and sales doubled.

◎ Ask, "Why not?" Almost everything you don't do has no good reason for it. Almost everything you don't do is the result of fear or inertia or a historical lack of someone asking, "Why not?"

BRAND AND COMPANY INDEX

WHAT WOULD ORWELL SAY?

A few clip-'n'-save slogans for you:

DON'T BE BORING

SAFE IS RISKY

DESIGN RULES NOW

VERY GOOD
IS BAD

About the author

Seth Godin is a professional speaker, a writer and an agent of change. He's the author of four worldwide bestsellers, all of which you can find at www.sethgodin.com. His other titles include *Permission Marketing, Unleashing the Ideavirus, The Big Red Fez* and *Survival Is Not Enough.*

Seth periodically hosts Purple Cow workshops at his loft outside of New York, and you can find details about attending one (or having one at your office) at sethgodin.com.

You can reach him by email at sethgodin@yahoo.com. He doesn't do consulting, but he does read all his mail.

More Information

To find out more information about Purple Cow, please visit www.apurplecow.com. No, it won't be a remarkable multimedia experience, but hey, it's free.

Is your company stuck? Enmeshed in a post-TV-Industrial-Complex funk? The only way to fix your company is to teach them about the Cow. Go ahead. Buy a book for everyone.

This book was designed by Red Maxwell and copyedited by Catherine E. Oliver. Special thanks to the Lark braintrust: Karen Watts, Lisa DiMona and Robin Dellabough. And to Julie Anixter, too. Helene & Alex Godin, Chris Meyer, Alan Webber, Bill Taylor and Lynn Gordon were kind enough to read the manuscript in the early stages. Michael Cader helped brainstorm our remarkable distribution strategy. Thanks!

The only reason you're holding the hardcover edition of *Purple Cow* in your hands is the hard work of Adrian Zackheim, Stephanie Land and Will Weisser at Portfolio. Thanks, guys!

As always, before this book was a book, it was a riff on my blog, and readers of my blog read it first. You can subscribe to my free blog (and find out what a blog is!) by visiting www.sethgodin.com. Just click on my head.

———

I Want to Share the News on how a company called bzzagent worked behind the scenes to promote this book, but that wouldn't be timely enough. Instead, visit www.apurplecow.com/bzz for the details.